FABULOUS

Parties

'Classy, elegant, beautiful... Mark's Garden'

Whoopi Goldberg

FABULOUS *Parties*

FOOD AND FLOWERS FOR
ELEGANT ENTERTAINING

MARK HELD, RICHARD DAVID & PEGGY DARK

RYLAND
PETERS
& SMALL

LONDON NEW YORK

Designer Pamela Daniels
Senior editor Julia Charles
Location research Peggy Dark, Mark Held
    and Richard David
Picture manager Emily Westlake
Production manager Patricia Harrington
Art director Leslie Harrington
Publishing director Alison Starling

Food stylists Valerie Aikman-Smith
    and Robyn Valerik
Mixologist Brent Sherman
Recipe writer Megan Slaughter

First published in the UK in 2008
by Ryland Peters & Small
20–21 Jockey's Fields
London WC1R 4BW
www.rylandpeters.com

10 9 8 7 6 5 4 3 2 1

ISBN 978 1 84597 627 9

Printed and bound in China.

Contents

Introduction

As the famous American hostess Elsa Maxwell said about
entertaining in the mid-twentienth century: 'Serve the dinner
backward, do anything — but for goodness sake, do something
weird.' It is still a good point. Attempt something new each
time your entertain.

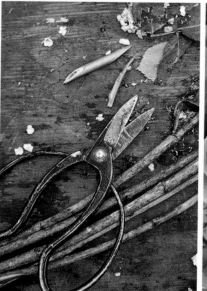

'Mark's Garden is like taking a peek into the Gardens of Babylon or, to go back a bit further, the Garden of Eden. I don't know where the flowers come from, but they have an unearthly quality. They are so crisp and alive and the colours are otherworldly. I wish I had their greenhouse, but thankfully they share it with me every season of the year. Whenever friends send me flowers from this haven of beauty I feel like I know what heaven must be like.'

Dame Elizabeth Taylor

opposite page
Richard and Mark at work.

Fresh Ideas for Entertaining

Los Angeles is not like other towns. In so many ways. For better or worse. Arguably, its cultural diversity is unsurpassed anywhere else in the world. Geographically, the terrain we call Los Angeles spans from the mountain foothills of Pasadena to the densely populated downtown, across The Valley, the canyons of Hollywood and Beverly Hills down to the famous beaches of Santa Monica and Malibu. The climate is one of the most pleasant in the world. Except for a few annoyances like traffic congestion, a little smog, and occasional earthquakes, we are very privileged.

Los Angeles has always been The Edge. It has always personified the pioneer spirit, searching for the new, breaking conventions and barriers. To its detriment at times, the old in Los Angeles has always taken backseat to the new. It's always about what's hot and what's the next big thing.

From the earliest beginnings everything here was newly invented. After all, this was basically a desert. The invention has had a lot to do with the original film industry that was built here. Los Angeles was a desolate town with no place to go, nothing to do. Those old time producers, directors, and movie stars not only invented motion pictures, they invented their own entertainment and their own way of living. It became a style that fascinated and influenced people and became emulated around the world. That public enthrallment has continued to this day making Los Angeles a permanent epicenter for entertainment and new trends of all kinds.

As they did from the very beginning people still flock to Los Angeles looking for their new world, new horizons, new adventures, new opportunities, new starts. A huge number of them have made good lives here. Los Angeles is home to some of the most successful, wealthiest, famous, most sophisticated people in the world. Many of these people are our clients and we love them. They give us the opportunity to create fabulous parties for them on a regular basis. It is a challenge to exercise our talents and push beyond normal limits to generate new concepts and styles. Few other places can offer this. Fortunately we have thrived on it. We have tried to give you a little taste of that in this book. We do not intend it to be an instructional guide but we are passing along a few secrets for giving a spectacular party and offer you some inspiration. 'Try something new' is our motto and we encourage you to experiment with different ideas each time you entertain. The parties in this book are all based on a theme. It's not mandatory to have a defined theme although that can be fun, but it is best to at least have a point of view in your mind. It's one of the easiest ways to start planning. It encourages you to focus on a look or a feel that can assist you in making

other selections. A sample starting point is to choose a type of food you want to serve or a motif or even just a colour. You might have a guest of honor who loves spicy food or pink. Maybe someone loves gardening or golf. These are good beginnings to help you plan.

One of the most critical elements of your event is, of course, the food. It must taste good and there must be plenty of it. Even if you are not preparing the quantities we produce at our parties, it helps to approach it the same way we do. If you are doing the cooking, limit the number of ingredients necessary and prepare as much as you can in advance, leaving finishing touches to a minimum.

As your guests gather, the momentum should begin immediately, and that is why we always allow a generous – but not overly extended – cocktail and hors d'oeuvres hour. Cocktails are back in a big way. We always try to create something unusual that fits into the theme of the affair and prepares the palate for the array of food that will follow. Hors d'oeuvres are something you can approach bravely with no-holds-barred. Tidbits of adventurous samplings not only whet the appetite before a meal, they offer entertainment to the palate so nobody makes a great commitment to a

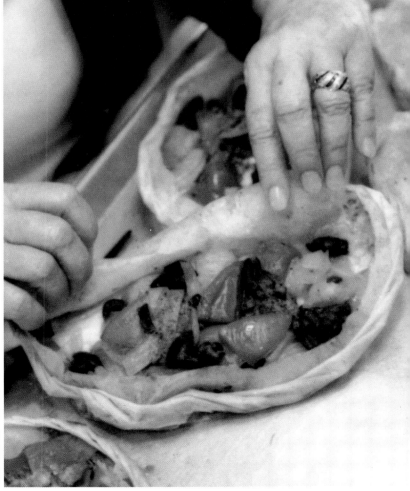

full portion of something. Most guests will try anything new in this way when they wouldn't imagine ordering it for a meal on a night out. Consequently this is really the time to try to give them something new and unexpected – our constant pursuit.

The food and the way it is presented expresses a lot about you, the host, and your regard for those you have gathered around you. A sumptuous feast is often the order of the night, especially for a holiday when most of us want to abandon our restricted diets and celebrate. Damn the waistline! Other events, however, call for a more subdued menu, such as the glorious salad bar we serve for our Pink Luncheon. It may be a light healthy meal, but there is such abundance to the choices that those of us who wish to indulge certainly get the opportunity to eat sumptuously.

Then there is dessert. What can we say about everybody's favourite food group? There is nothing we like better than seeing eyes light up when the desserts are brought out. For most of us they are so hard to resist and it is such a fun part of the affair that we will indulge ourselves, even if we share or just take a tidbit. Or two. We think it is important to always prepare desserts that look as good as they taste because half of the fun is looking. We feel that desserts are so important we created a party around our favourites!

Now the experienced host knows that food shares the stage with flowers at a successful party. Flowers set the mood as they lend an air of fun, sophistication, and festivity. The presence of flowers tells your guests that they are special and that you have gone to great effort to make them feel so. Flowers also help to establish the theme of your party since they can be so expressive in the way they are presented. They are an extension of the enjoyment of the food giving visual pleasure along with the sweet and savoury tastes of your menu.

Never underestimate the effect of flowers generally. After all of these years in the business, we are still surprised sometimes at the power flowers can have over people. Like one of our friends who hosts dozens of parties large and small every year has said, 'Whenever I send your flowers to people, they like me better.' And then she usually adds 'You're amazing!' What she really means is that flowers are amazing. She, like most experienced hostesses, would not think of entertaining without flowers surrounding her and her guests. The concept works. Flowers can transform people. They set the scene of a party like nothing else can.

Combined with a careful selection of details like invitations, table settings and lighting you can establish a mood that captures your guests' imaginations and lends your party a life of its own. It's also important to remember that no party is perfect. There are always a few small glitches. Don't worry if something goes wrong. Just move on and enjoy your own party and your guests will enjoy it too.

The Parties

To paraphrase the lyrics of a show-business anthem, just remember: 'Your party is a stage and the stage is a world of entertainment!' When you entertain always make sure it's truly entertaining!

An Elegant Dinner

MENU FOR 8 GUESTS

APERITIF   Aviation Cocktail

TO BE PASSED   South African Peppadews

With Goats' Cheese Filling

Beetroot Tartar with Feta Cheese

Served on Crispy Spoon-shaped Crackers

STARTER   Fillet of Sea Bass 'en Papillote'

With Lemon Kalamata Olive Butter and

Tomato and Basil Confit

Served with a basket of crispies, to include 'The Kitchen's' Cheese Toast

and Filo Pastry Twists

MAIN COURSE   Loin of Lamb

With Fresh Mint Pistou, Lemon Beurre Blanc and a Baby Vegetable Mélange

Served with a basket of assorted bread rolls

DESSERT   Pineapple Carpaccio

With Basil Gelato and Toasted Hazelnuts

right Lily of the valley surrounded
by sprigs of hydrangea in vintage
silver is one of the several small
pieces placed around the table.

Dinner by Candlelight

For a truly special occasion we often want to create an opulent and sumptuous affair to demonstrate to our guest of honour and our guests just how important we believe they are.

For this dinner we pulled out all the stops and loaded the table with a lavish array of all white flowers and fine china, crystal and silver. The setting is, appropriately, the former estate of Virginia Robinson, known as the 'First Lady of Beverly Hills' in the mid-twentieth century. She was famous for her extravagant parties attended by the world's elite, including famous movie stars of the period like Fred Astaire and Charles Boyer. Now a museum bequeathed to Los Angeles County, the historic home is filled with her treasures and the fabulous grounds still possess wonderful gardens that we attempted to emulate indoors.

Two statuesque candelabras mounted with huge arrangements of white garden roses, peonies, dahlias and hydrangea command the table and rise high above the guests' heads, twining into the overhead crystal chandelier. Down the length of the table, below the guests' eye level, clusters of mixed vintage silver containers are filled with more garden roses, lily of the valley and sweet peas and each folded linen napkin is decorated with a dainty nosegay of white lavender which is braided with delicate white satin ribbon. The sparkling crystal and silver are complemented by jewel-studded place cards with each guest's name inscribed in graceful calligraphy.

Of course we also include as many decorative votive candles as we can fit on the table to cast a flattering golden glow on the happy faces of our special guests.

left Each folded napkin is studded with a nosegay of white lavender braided with delicate ribbon.

right An Aviation Cocktail served in a Martini glass perfectly complements this elegant table setting.

Aviation Cocktail

MAKES 1 DRINK

50 ml gin
25 ml maraschino liqueur
1 tablespoon freshly squeezed lemon juice
a twist of lemon zest, to garnish

Shake all the ingredients over ice and strain into a chilled Martini glass. Garnish with the lemon zest.

South African Peppadews with Goats' Cheese Filling

MAKES 24 OR MORE APPETIZERS

24 pickled peppadews (or other pickled sweet red pepper), drained
250 g soft goats' cheese
50 g finely chopped chives

Drain the peppadews and fill each one with a teaspoon or more of goats' cheese. Sprinkle with chives. The filled peppadews may be covered and refrigerated for up to 2 hours before serving.

Beetroot Tartar with Feta Cheese

MAKES 24 OR MORE APPETIZERS

450 g uncooked beetroot, scrubbed and rinsed
6 tablespoons olive oil
2–3 tablespoons white balsamic vinegar
1 tablespoon Dijon mustard
2 shallots, finely minced
3 tablespoons chopped chives
2 teaspoons dried chilli flakes
200 g feta cheese
sea salt and freshly ground black pepper
5 sprigs thyme, leaves removed, for garnish
24 Crispy Spoon-shaped Crackers, to serve (see page 144) or other crackers
aluminum foil

Preheat the oven to 220°C (425°F) Gas 7. Toss the beetroot with 3 tablespoons of the oil and a little salt. Wrap the beetroot in foil and place them on a baking tray.

Bake in the preheated oven until they can be easily pierced with a fork, about 1 hour. When cool enough to handle, peel and cut into small dice. Combine the remaining 3 tablespoons oil, vinegar, mustard, shallots, chives and dried chilli flakes. Toss the cooked beetroot in the dressing and season to taste with salt and pepper.

Place a teaspoon of feta on a Crispy Spoon-shaped Cracker. Top with a tablespoon of the dressed beetroot. Garnish with a little fresh thyme and serve immediately.

Preheat the oven to 180°C (350°F) Gas 4. Place the packages on baking trays, making sure they are not touching each other. Allow enough space for the paper to puff up. Bake in the preheated oven for 10–12 minutes or until golden brown. Using scissors, cut open the packages in the uncrimped portion. Remove the cooked herbs. Add fresh sprigs of herbs, a little more Lemon Kalamata Olive Butter and a lemon wedge.

Note: The 'papillote' is an easy prepared starter. If you want to serve it as a main course, a few cooked baby new potatoes can be added to the package as you prepare them. After the packages are opened, tuck in steamed asparagus spears or haricot vert.

TOMATO AND BASIL CONFIT

Makes 950 ml

1 medium yellow onion, roughly chopped
3 tablespoons olive oil
600–650 g ripe heirloom tomatoes, peeled
    and chopped
250 g pitted black olives, chopped
140 g capers
a large handful of basil, finely chopped
coarse salt and freshly ground black pepper

In a sauté pan over medium heat, sauté the onion in oil until translucent. Remove from the heat and transfer to a large bowl. Add the tomatoes, olives, capers, and basil and season to taste with salt and pepper.

LEMON KALAMATA OLIVE BUTTER

Makes about 400 g

230 g butter
2 tablespoons finely grated lemon zest
100 g pitted black kalamata olives, chopped
4 tablespoons thyme or savory, finely chopped

Combine all the ingredients in a food processor and blend until well combined. The butter will keep for 2–3 days in a sealable air-tight container and refrigerated for 2–3 days. Allow to soften before using.

Note: The butter is also food for finishing potatoes or cooked vegetables. Melt a pat on the hot food and toss gently to coat.

Fillet of Sea Bass 'en Papillote' with Lemon Kalamata Olive Butter and Tomato and Basil Confit

SERVES 8

125 ml olive oil
8 sea bass, sole or snapper fillets, 175–200 g each
Heirloom Tomato and Basil Confit (see right)
Lemon Kalamata Olive Butter (see right), or
    black truffle oil
2 eggs, beaten with 3 tablespoons cold water
sea salt and freshly ground black pepper
16 sprigs thyme, savory or chervil, to garnish
8 pieces of greaseproof paper, 30 x 35 cm,
    folded and cut into ½ hearts

Open out the greaseproof paper heart. Brush with olive oil and season with salt and pepper. Place a fish fillet on the right-hand side of the heart and top with 2 tablespoons each of Heirloom Tomato Confit and Lemon Kalamata Olive Butter, or brush with a little black truffle oil.

Fold the left-hand side over the fish and, starting at the top of the heart shape, fold both edges of the paper together to seal, overlapping the folds as you move along. Secure the package by sharply twisting the end. Brush the outside of the package with the egg wash. Refrigerate until ready to bake. Repeat with the remaining fish fillets.

Loin of Lamb with Fresh Mint Pistou, Lemon Beurre Blanc and a Baby Vegetable Mélange
(see photograph on page 22)

SERVES 8

olive oil, to sear

140–175 g boneless loin of lamb per guest, cleaned and trimmed

50 g butter

280 g broad beans, cleaned and blanched

280 g baby radishes, cut in half vertically

280 g asparagus tips, blanched

280 g green and yellow baby summer squash, cut in half and blanched

350 g small new or marble potatoes, blanched

sea salt and freshly ground black pepper

fresh green herbs of your choice, to garnish

To serve:

Fresh Mint Pistou (optional)

Lemon Beurre Blanc (optional)

Preheat the oven to 190°C (375°F) Gas 5. Heat sufficient olive oil in a frying pan and sear the lamb fillets. Season with salt and pepper. Transfer to a roasting tin and cook in the preheated oven for 20–25 minutes, or until a thermometer inserted in the meat reads 43–46°C. Remove from the oven and let rest for at least 5 minutes.

Melt the butter in a large frying pan. Add the vegetables and sauté until heated through and tender. Distribute the vegetables between 8 serving plates and top each with 3–4 slices of the lamb. Spoon a little Lemon Beurre Blanc over each serving, if using. Garnish with fresh herbs and serve with a dish of Mint Pistou for passing, if desired.

FRESH MINT PISTOU
Makes 450 ml

450 g mint leaves

125 g parsley, coarsely chopped

2 garlic cloves

125 g grated Parmesan or Asiago cheese

50 g pine nuts

olive oil to taste

finely grated zest of 1 unwaxed lemon

freshly squeezed lemon juice, to taste

sea salt and freshly ground black pepper

Place the herbs, garlic, cheese and pine nuts in a food processor. While running, slowly add olive oil until the pistou has the desired consistency. Season with salt and pepper. Add lemon juice and zest to taste.

LEMON BEURRE BLANC
Makes 175 ml

125 ml dry white wine

50 g shallots, very finely chopped

3 tablespoons freshly squeezed lemon juice

2 tablespoons thick whipping cream

50 g unsalted butter, cubed

1½ teaspoons finely grated lemon zest

sea salt and freshly ground black pepper

Put the wine and shallots in a saucepan with the lemon juice. Bring to the boil over medium/high heat, and let reduce to about 150 ml. Add the cream and continue to boil gently until thickened, about 5 minutes.

Remove the pan from the heat and add the butter a few cubes at a time, whisking until just melted and incorporated into the sauce. Stir in the lemon zest and season to taste with salt and pepper. Keep warm until ready to serve.

Pineapple Carpaccio with Basil Gelato and Toasted Hazelnuts
SERVES 8–10

1 fresh pineapple, peeled

250 g toasted hazelnuts

For the gelato:

450 ml whole milk

250 ml double cream

350 g granulated sugar

75 g basil, chopped

8 egg yolks

an ice cream maker

2 baking trays lined with greaseproof paper

To make the gelato, put the milk, cream and 250 g of the sugar in a large saucepan. Bring to the boil, stirring constantly. Remove the pan from the heat and add the chopped basil immediately. Let the mixture steep for 1 hour or more.

Beat the egg yolks and remaining sugar with an electric mixer until pale yellow. Add the milk mixture and heat in a double boiler, whisking constantly until the mixture thickens. Remove from the heat and pass through a nylon sieve. Chill for several hours or overnight. Follow the manufacturer's instructions for your ice cream maker to finish the ice cream.

To make the Pineapple Carpaccio preheat the oven to 150°C (300°F) Gas 2. Slice the pineapple as thinly as possible using an electric slicer or mandoline. Lay out on baking trays lined with greaseproof paper. Place in the preheated oven for 15–25 minutes, turning occasionally, until dry, but still pliable.

To serve, fold a slice of pineapple into a cup or flower shape. Add a scoop of the basil gelato and sprinkle with toasted hazelnuts. Serve immediately.

An Asian Inspired Dinner

MENU FOR 6-8 GUESTS

APERITIF — Double Happiness

TO BE PASSED — Wild Mushroom Gyoza
With Spicy Thai Sauce

Sashimi Salmon Rice Rolls
With Wasabi Caviar

STARTER — Spicy Asian Coleslaw
With Crispy Fried Ginger and Peanuts

MAIN COURSE — Fillet of Sea Bass in a Ti Leaf Package
With Ponzu Sauce and Sautéed Red and Yellow Peppers

Served with a Steamed Jasmine Rice

Three Pea Mélange
With Orange Zest

DESSERT — Ginger Tartlets
With Crystallized Ginger

'When it comes to flowers, Mark's Garden is the one place Hollywood turns
to for that perfect blend of elegance, imagination, and allure, making
their creations so unforgettable.'

Bonnie Tiegel
Producer for Entertainment Tonight

A Tranquil Mood

Much like the art of 'bonsai' which originated in China but has become associated with Japan, our Asian party is a blend of Far Eastern motifs and foods. Our objective was to establish a tranquil, Zen-like mood for which we adopted the yin-yang balance of black and white and the natural green hues of nature. The trick is to maintain a calm simplicity in the design but to establish a festive enough ambience that guests still feel they are at a party. We think these two fanciful handmade bonsai trees arching over the table set the perfect tone.

The bonsai trees are made of found tree branches with clumps of Ming greenery attached in bonsai-style clusters. At their feet are mood moss and our signature 'glamellias', which for this theme are composed of green cymbidium orchid petals. At first glance a glamellia resembles an oversized natural bloom but it is actually a handmade blossom painstakingly created by attaching individual petals to a central base, most often plastic foam. You will see other versions of this 'flower' included in some of our other parties.

A bold patterned black and white runner is a nice blend of simple style and flamboyance to add vitality to the room. Elegant 'black' and white calla lilies packed into alternating black and white square glass vases are placed down the centre of the table. Some of the calla lily stems are wrapped around the outside of the vase and secured with decorative twine. Votive candles are wrapped in large white calla lily petals and tied with lengths of thin black ribbon. Some small decorative Buddha heads have been placed on the table and each guest's name is written in Japanese script on a place card at each setting to further embody the Asian character of the party.

Double Happiness

MAKES 6-8 DRINKS

125 ml sake
125 ml fresh peach juice
   or 100 ml peach nectar mixed with 1 fl oz. water
fresh peach slices, to garnish

Pour the sake and peach juice into
a cocktail shaker filled with plenty of
ice. Shake to combine then strain into
chilled cocktail glasses. Garnish each one
with a peach slice and serve immediately.

Wild Mushroom Gyoza with Spicy Thai Sauce

MAKES 35 PIECES

50 ml vegetable or chicken stock,
   plus 5 tablespoons
100 ml oyster sauce
3 tablespoons soy sauce
2 tablespoons unseasoned rice vinegar
2½ tablespoons dry sherry
½ teaspoon sugar
⅛ teaspoon freshly ground black pepper
3-4 tablespoons corn oil, for stir-frying
1 tablespoon finely grated fresh ginger
2 tablespoons finely minced garlic
1 yellow onion, finely diced
2 shallots, minced
900 g mixed mushrooms, very finely diced
30 chives, finely chopped
10 spring onions, thinly sliced
3 tablespoons cornflour
35 wonton wrappers

120 ml corn or vegetable oil, for deep frying
Spicy Thai Sauce, to serve

Put 60 ml stock plus the next 6 ingredients
in a bowl and whisk to combine. Set aside
until needed.

In a large frying pan, heat 3 tablespoons oil
and add the ginger and garlic. Sauté over
medium/low heat for about 30 seconds.
Add the onion and shallots and continue to
sauté for 2 minutes more, or until the onions
are translucent. Add the mushrooms and
sauté for another 2-3 minutes, adding more
oil if needed. Add the chives and spring
onions and stir in the ingredients in the bowl.
Bring to a simmer. Mix the remaining stock
with the cornflour and add to the frying pan.
Stir constantly and bring back to the boil to
thicken the mushroom mixture. When thick,
remove from heat and allow to cool.

Lay out the wonton wrappers and place a
tablespoon of the mushroom mixture in the
centre of each one. Brush the edges of
the wonton wrappers with water, fold in half
and press the ends together to seal. Heat
the oil in a deep, lidded frying pan. Place
the gyoza in the pan and brown the bottoms
only. Reduce the heat to medium/low, spray
the tops of gyoza with water or add 50 ml
water. Cover and steam for a minute or two
until completely cooked. Serve immediately
with Spicy Thai sauce.

SPICY THAI SAUCE

Makes 600 ml

175 ml corn oil
125 ml rice vinegar
125 ml teriyaki glaze
50 ml soy sauce
50 ml sesame oil
2 tablespoons sugar
Sambal or other hot sauce, to taste
finely chopped fresh chives, to serve (optional)

Put all of the ingredients in a bowl and
whisk to combine. The dressing will keep
in a sealed jar for 2-3 weeks, refrigerated.
Shake to combine ingredients before using
and add a few chives just before serving.

Sashimi Salmon Rice Rolls with Wasabi Caviar

MAKES 32 APPETIZERS

8 rice paper wrappers
400-450 g wild salmon fillet
250 g ready-made wasabi caviar (optional)
3-4 spring onions, cut into 5-cm lengths
bottled plum sauce or sweet chilli sauce, to serve

For the filling:

125 g carrots, cut into thin matchsticks
125 g jicama or daikon, cut into thin matchsticks
50 g coriander, finely chopped
2 tablespoons chopped mint
50 ml bottled plum sauce or sweet chili sauce
1 tablespoon sesame oil
3 tablespoons Thai or Vietnamese fish sauce
2 tablespoons grated fresh ginger

2 tablespoons chopped roasted and salted peanuts
50 ml freshly squeezed lime juice
32 coriander sprigs, to garnish

Cut each rice paper wrapper into quarters and cut off the rounded edges. Slice the salmon as thinly as possible using a very sharp knife. Combine all the filling ingredients, saving the coriander sprigs. Soak the rice paper squares in water until pliable then pat dry. Place a coriander sprig on a rice paper square, top with salmon and a tablespoon of the filling mixture. Roll up tightly like a cigar. Garnish each roll with a teaspoon of wasabi caviar, if using, and a spring onion length. Serve with plum sauce or sweet chilli sauce for dipping.

Spicy Asian Coleslaw
SERVES 8-10
freshly squeezed juice of 1 orange
freshly squeezed juice of 2 limes
1 tablespoon sugar
2 tablespoons rice vinegar
50 ml vegetable oil
a pinch of sea salt
3 tablespoons bottled sweet chilli sauce
1 tablespoon hot sauce, or to taste
1 head Chinese leaves, finely shredded
1 medium head red cabbage, shredded
½ head Savoy cabbage, shredded
2 medium carrots, grated
½ jicama or daikon, cut into thin matchsticks
4 small cucumbers, thinly sliced
125 g mint leaves, cut into strips

175 g pickled ginger, well drained
175 g salted peanuts
oil, for shallow frying

To make the dressing put the first 8 ingredients in a small bowl and whisk to combine. Place the Chinese leaves, red cabbage, Savoy cabbage, carrots, jicama, cucumbers and mint in a large salad bowl. Heat a little oil in a wok. Fry the ginger until crispy. Remove from the pan with a slotted spoon and drain on kitchen paper.

To assemble the salad, add the fried ginger and peanuts to the cabbage mixture, pour in the dressing and toss the salad to distribute evenly. Serve immediately.

Fillet of Sea Bass in a Ti Leaf Package with Ponzu Sauce and Sautéed Red and Yellow Peppers
SERVES 8
9 fresh Ti leaves (or banana leaf if not available)
8 x 175-200 g sea bass or halibut fillets
3 red and yellow peppers, cut into matchsticks
2 tablespoons olive oil
sea salt and freshly ground black pepper
450 ml Ponzu Sauce, to serve (see right)
steamed jasmine rice, to serve (optional)

Simmer the Ti leaves in a large pan of boiling water until pliable. Pat dry with kitchen paper. Pull a leaf into 8 long shreds and set aside with the remaining leaves.

Lightly sauté the peppers in olive oil. Season the fish fillets and lightly brown on both sides under a hot grill. On each Ti leaf, place a fish fillet 50 ml Ponzu Sauce, and a few sautéed red and yellow peppers. Fold and wrap each Ti leaf to form a package and tie shut with one of the Ti leaf shreds. Refrigerate until ready to cook.

Preheat the oven to 190°C (375°F) Gas 5. Spread the Ti leaf and fish packages on baking trays. Bake in the preheated oven for 25 minutes, or until the fish is tender and the leaf slightly browned. Serve with steamed jasmine rice and additional Ponzu Sauce for pouring.

PONZU SAUCE

Makes 450 ml

4 tablespoons freshly squeezed lemon juice

125 ml rice vinegar

6 tablespoons soy sauce

2 tablespoons mirin (sweet cooking sake) or dry sherry

freshly grated zest of 2 unwaxed lemon

Combine all the ingredients in a saucepan and bring to the boil, stirring continuously. Let cool and refrigerate until needed.

Three Pea Mélange with Orange Zest

SERVES 8

450 g shelled fresh or defrosted frozen peas

450 g sugar snaps, trimmed

450 g mangetout, trimmed

2 tablespoons olive oil or butter

50 ml freshly squeezed orange juice

sea salt and freshly ground black pepper

2 tablespoons freshly grated orange zest

In a large frying pan, heat the oil or butter. Add the peas, sugar snaps and mangetout and sauté for 1–2 minutes. Add the orange juice and continue to sauté until heated through but still a little crunchy. Season with salt and pepper. Sprinkle with orange zest to serve.

Ginger Tartlets

MAKES 8 INDIVIDUAL TARTLETS

For the tartlet shell:

450 g shortbread biscuits, crushed into fine crumbs

125 g sugar

freshly grated zest from 2 unwaxed lemons

85 g cold unsalted butter, cut into pieces

2 teaspoons ground ginger

For the filling:

4 tablespoons whole milk

3 teaspoons unflavoured powdered gelatin

250 g finely chopped crystallized ginger, plus a little extra cut into matchsticks, to garnish

125 g sugar

2 teaspoons freshly squeezed lemon juice

1½ teaspoons salt

1 litre double cream

360 ml crème fraîche

8 x 12-cm round loose-bottomed tartlet tins

Preheat the oven to 180°C (350°F) Gas 4. To make the tartlet shells, combine the shortbread crumbs, sugar, lemon zest, butter and ginger in a food processor until it starts to come together. Line the tartlet tins with the dough, pressing it down on the base and into the sides. Place on baking trays and bake in the preheated oven for 15 minutes, until golden. Remove from the oven and set aside to cool.

To make the filling, put the milk in a bowl, sprinkle the gelatin over the top, and let it soften. Transfer the mixture to a saucepan and cook with the ginger, sugar, lemon juice, salt and half the cream. Stir over medium heat until the gelatin and sugar are dissolved. Remove from the heat and let cool to room temperature.

In a large bowl, whisk the crème fraîche until it is smooth. Whip the remaining cream to soft peaks and gently fold into the crème fraîche. Gently fold the ginger milk mixture into the whipped cream until combined. Spoon the mixture into the tart shells and chill in the refrigerator until set.

When ready to serve, carefully remove the tartlets from the tins and sprinkle the top of each one with a little crystallized ginger.

A Summertime Lunch

MENU FOR 6-8 GUESTS

APERITIF   Fresh Peach Fuzz

STARTER   Chilled Tomato Soup
Served in glasses and with Basil Oil and Fresh Basil Garnish

MAIN COURSE   Cheddar Cheese Soufflés
Served with Cheddar Cheese Sauce with White Truffle Oil

DESSERT   Red Berry Romanoff
With Grand Marnier Romanoff Sauce

Lace Cookies

right Big, luscious hydrangea blooms float in glass lanterns hanging from the tree limbs. *below right* Passion flower blooms add an exotic touch.

Summer Breeze

To escape the summer heat our summertime lunch is set at a long table on the lawn under a sprawling shade tree. To complement our light summer menu we have chosen a colour palette predominantly of blues to provide a cool, soothing environment. After enjoying a frosty Peach Fuzz drink or a glass of icy lemonade on the veranda, our guests will move to the table bathed in a sea of shimmering blue and lavender flowers to settle in for an afternoon of 'easy living'.

Every blue and lavender flower we could lay our hands on is incorporated into this tabletop to soothe the soul and please the senses. Hydrangea provides us with a wonderful variety of blue tones to which we have added hyacinth, muscari, a few purple callas and tulips and one of our favourites straight from the garden – passion vine. This is all generously spread out over a patterned tablecloth to match the expected mood of the gathering. The chair backs are also treated with hydrangea and the big, luscious blooms float in glass lanterns hanging from the tree limbs. As a party favour guests will take home the loose nosegays that adorn the silver epergne in the centre of the table.

Fresh Peach Fuzz

MAKES 4-6 DRINKS

175 ml container frozen lemonade
    concentrate (do not dilute)
175 ml gin or vodka
2–3 ripe peaches, unpeeled and sliced
4–5 ice cubes
mint sprigs to garnish

Combine all the ingredients in a blender,
saving some peach slices to garnish. Purée
at high speed until smooth. Adjust to taste.
Garnish with mint and the reserved peach
slices. Serve immediately.

Chilled Tomato Soup

SERVES 8-10

1.8 kg ripe plum tomatoes
8 cloves garlic, peeled
leaves from 4 sprigs of thyme
100 ml olive oil
2 cucumbers, peeled and chopped
125 g sun-dried tomatoes in olive oil
½ litre chicken or vegetable stock
sea salt and freshly ground black pepper
basil oil and basil leaves, to garnish
2 baking trays with a rim or Swiss roll tins
8–10 Martini glasses or similar

Preheat the oven to 180°C (350°F) Gas 4.
Chop the tomatoes and combine with
the garlic and thyme. Toss in olive oil
and spread on the baking trays. Roast in
the preheated oven for 45–60 minutes.
Remove from the oven and allow to cool.

Put the cooked tomatoes, cucumbers
and sun-dried tomatoes in a food
processor. Blend to a purée and add
the stock. Season to taste with salt and
pepper. Chill for several hours or overnight.

Serve in Martini glasses, drizzled with basil
oil and garnished with a little fresh basil.

Cheddar Cheese Soufflés

SERVES 8-10

3 tablespoons unsalted butter, plus extra
    for greasing
65 g Parmesan cheese, finely grated,
    plus extra for sprinkling
30 g plain flour
250 ml hot milk
a pinch of cayenne pepper
a pinch of nutmeg
4 extra large egg yolks, at room temperature
140 g mature Cheddar cheese, grated
5 extra large egg whites, at room temperature
⅛ teaspoon cream of tartar
sea salt and freshly ground black pepper
8–10 individual soufflé dishes or ramekins

Preheat the oven to 190°C (375°F) Gas 5.
Butter the soufflé dishes and sprinkle
with Parmesan. Melt the butter in a small
saucepan over low heat. Stir in the flour
and cook for 2 minutes, stirring constantly.
Remove from the heat, whisk in the hot
milk, ½ teaspoon each of salt and pepper,
the cayenne and nutmeg. Cook over low
heat, beating constantly, for 1 minute until
the mixture is smooth and thick.

Remove from the heat. While still hot, whisk
in the egg yolks, one at a time. Stir in the
Cheddar and Parmesan cheeses. Transfer to
a large bowl.

In a separate bowl, use an electric whisk to
whisk the egg whites, cream of tartar and
a pinch of salt on low speed for 1 minute,
medium for 1 minute, and then high, until
they form firm, glossy peaks.

Whisk half the egg whites into the cheese
mixture to lighten it, then fold in the rest.
Pour into the prepared soufflé dishes. Bake
in the preheated oven for 30–35 minutes
until puffed and brown. Serve immediately
with warm Cheddar Cheese Sauce with
White Truffle Oil.

CHEDDAR CHEESE SAUCE WITH WHITE TRUFFLE OIL

Makes about 1 litre

60 g butter
30 g plain flour
600 ml whole milk
1 teaspoon Worcestershire sauce
450 g mature Cheddar cheese, grated
1-2 teaspoons white truffle oil, plus extra
   to season
salt and freshly ground black pepper

In a medium saucepan, melt the butter and stir in the flour. Cook over low heat for about 2 minutes, until a golden brown. Remove from the heat and add the milk, Worcestershire sauce, cheese and white truffle oil. Return to the heat and stir continuously until the cheese has melted and all the ingredients have combined to make a smooth sauce. Season to taste with salt, pepper, and a little more truffle oil if desired. Serve warm or gently reheat before serving.

Red Berry Romanoff

SERVES 8-10

250 g each of blueberries, blackberries,
   raspberries and strawberries
125 g granulated sugar
60 ml Grand Marnier
Grand Marnier Romanoff Sauce, to serve
Lace Biscuits, to serve (optional)

8-10 individual serving glasses

Rinse all of the berries and hull and slice the strawberries. Put them in a large bowl, sprinkle with sugar and pour in the Grand Marnier. Stir gently to coat and set aside to let the sugar dissolve in the Grand Marnier.

When ready to serve, spoon a generous amount of berries into serving glasses. Top with Grand Marnier Romanoff Sauce and garnish with a Lace Cookie, if desired.

GRAND MARNIER ROMANOFF SAUCE

Makes about 1 litre

6 egg yolks
250 g granulated sugar
350 ml double cream
60 ml Grand Marnier liqueur

Put the egg yolks in a metal mixing bowl and whisk. Slowly whisk in the sugar until the mixture is a pale yellow and the sugar has dissolved. Place the mixture over a double boiler, and whisk over low heat until thick. Let cool.

Put the cream in a large bowl and whip to stiff peaks. Fold the whipped cream and Grand Marnier into the cooled egg and sugar mixture.

Note: At the The Kitchen we also serve this sauce as a dip with a platter of fresh fruit.

Lace Cookies

SERVES 8-10

125 g unsalted butter
125 g granulated sugar
100 ml golden syrup
60 g plain flour
1 teaspoon ground ginger
½ teaspoon salt
a baking tray, lightly greased

Preheat the oven to 190°C (375°F) Gas 5.
Put the butter, sugar and golden syrup in
a saucepan and cook over medium heat,
stirring continuously, for 4 minutes. Add the
flour, ginger and salt and whisk or stir until
well combined. Remove from the heat and
let cool. Transfer the mixture to a storage
container and chill in the refrigerator for
several hours or until set.

Once set, use two teaspoons or a small
ce cream scoop to transfer mounds of the
mixture to the prepared baking tray. Bake
until the mixture spreads and is golden
brown, about 15 minutes. Let cool slightly
but, while still warm, cut or mould into
desired shapes.

The cookies will keep for up to 1 week
stored in an airtight container. Use as a
garnish for Red Berry Romanoff with
Grand Marnier Romanoff sauce or serve
with ice cream.

below Even the lemonade station
that stands nearby is circled with
hydrangea and tufts of muscari,
giving our guests the feeling they
are swept by a cooling breeze.

A Chic Cocktail Party

MENU FOR 6–8 GUESTS

APERITIF   Cucumber Basil Gimlet

Pear Side-car

TO BE PASSED   Ahi Tuna Tartar
On a Wonton Crisp with Wasabi Sauce

Warm Brie in a Crispy Cup
With White Truffle Honey and Toasted Almonds

Chicken Tonnato
Served on a Crostini

Beef Carpaccio
With Rosemary Aïoli

Crispy Fried Olives
Stuffed with Sausage and Goats' Cheese

DESSERT   Mini Lemon Millefeuilles

High Style

The British invented the cocktail party (reportedly the author Alec Waugh in the 1920s) but it was probably the Americans who really perfected the art of cocktail mixing. Apparently during the Prohibition period mixing spirits with other liquids disguised the horrible flavour of bootleg alcohol. Although once out of fashion, cocktails today are more stylish than ever and from that we take our cue to raise the art of the cocktail party to the highest level of chic. Elegant black and white with a splash of yellow is what we have chosen to establish a mood of sophistication along with the unexpected.

Because yellow is an 'edgy' colour and works well as an accent, we like this combination along with the perfect complacency of black and white. Sleek, stark and sophisticated, this is a dramatic setting for the most glamorous array of guests. Even the most modest can feel exceptional in this environment. Masses of black calla lilies, yellow freesia and yellow craspedia balls accented with large tropical leaves and trimmed horsetail become sculptural art pieces in this gorgeous showcase of light and shadow. Can't you just imagine Audrey Hepburn standing in the corner in a black cocktail dress?

Cucumber Basil Gimlet

MAKES 1 DRINK

75 ml gin
15 ml lime cordial (Rose's or Angostura)
5 basil leaves, torn
5 cucumber slices, chopped
cucumber spear, to garnish

Put all the ingredients into a cocktail shaker.
Add ice and shake to chill. Strain into a
chilled glass and garnish with a cucumber
spear. Serve immediately.

Pear Side-car
MAKES 1 DRINK
30 ml brandy
30 ml pear brandy
25 ml freshly squeezed lemon juice
sugar, to serve
thin slice of pear, to garnish

Pour all the ingredients into a cocktail
shaker. Add ice and shake to chill. Strain
into a sugar-rimmed cocktail glass and
garnish with a slice of pear.

Ahi Tuna Tartar

MAKES 20 PIECES

5 wonton wrappers or skins, cut into quarters
125 ml good-quality mayonnaise
2 tablespoons wasabi powder
175 g sashimi grade ahi tuna
1 teaspoon sesame oil
3 dashes Tabasco sauce, or to taste
2 tablespoons finely chopped chives,
    plus extra to garnish
oil, for frying
sea salt and freshly ground black pepper

Heat the oil in a wok to 180°C. Fry the quartered wonton wrappers until very light brown, 3–5 seconds. Drain on kitchen paper. (You can do this in advance and keep the wrappers in an airtight container.)

To make the wasabi sauce, put the mayonnaise and wasabi powder in a bowl and whisk to combine. To make the tuna tartar, finely chop the tuna and put it in a bowl. Add the sesame oil, Tabasco and salt and pepper to taste. Add the chives and mix. Put a small amount of wasabi sauce on each wonton crisp, then spoon on a small mound of the tuna tartar. Garnish each with a few chopped chives and serve immediately.

Warm Brie in a Crispy Cup

MAKES 20 PIECES

5 wonton skins
125 g butter, melted
250 g ripe brie
2 tablespoons white truffle honey
60 g toasted flaked almonds
3-cm diameter cookie cutter
2 x 12-hole cupcake tins

Preheat the oven to 180°C (350°F) Gas 4. Cut 3-cm rounds out of the wonton skins (cut 4 from each skin). Brush each with melted butter and place in the cupcake tins.

Bake in the preheated oven for 8–10 minutes or until light brown. Remove the cups from the oven and fill each one with about 1 teaspoon of brie. Return to the oven and bake for a further 5 minutes or until the cheese has melted. Remove from the oven, drizzle with white truffle honey and top with almonds. Serve immediately.

Chicken Tonnato

MAKES 20 PIECES

1 tin (200–250 g) tuna in oil, preferably
    Spanish or Italian
2 tablespoons small capers, drained
375 ml good-quality mayonnaise
3 tablespoons freshly squeezed lemon juice
3 tinned anchovies
a pinch of cayenne pepper
20 prepared crostini or small square crackers
2 x 150-g grilled or poached chicken breasts,
    thinly sliced, about 3 mm thick
basil oil, to drizzle
basil leaves, chiffonade or julienned, to garnish
sea salt and freshly ground black pepper

Put the tuna, capers, mayonnaise, lemon juice, anchovies and cayenne in a food processor. Process until well combined and season to taste with salt and pepper.

Spoon about a teaspoon of the tuna mixture onto each crostini and top with a couple of slices of chicken. Drizzle with basil oil. Garnish with small basil leaves or finely chopped basil and serve immediately.

Crispy Fried Olives

MAKES 36 OLIVES

450 g sweet or spicy Italian sausage,
    casing removed
250 g firm goats' cheese, crumbled
1 tablespoon finely chopped flat leaf parsley
36 large brine-cured green olives, stoned
125 g plain flour
3 large eggs, beaten
250 g Panko or other dried breadcrumbs
oil, for frying
a piping bag fitted with very small nozzle

Heat some oil in a frying pan. Sauté the sausage then drain the excess oil. Transfer the cooked sausage to a bowl and add the goats' cheese and parsley. Mix to combine and spoon into a piping bag. The nozzle used should be small enough to fit into an olive. Stuff each olive with the mixture.

Put the flour, eggs and Panko into separate bowls. Taking a few stuffed olives at a time, coat them in the flour. Remove and coat completely in the beaten eggs, then remove and coat in Panko.

Heat some oil to 190°C in a wok or electric deep-fryer. Fry the olives until golden brown. Drain on kitchen paper and serve hot.

VARIATION
250 g goats' cheese
250 g aged asiago cheese
250 g cream cheese

Mix well and use to stuff the olives, then coat and fry as above.

Beef Carpaccio with Rosemary Aïoli
MAKES 25 PIECES
250–300 g best beef fillet
olive oil, to drizzle
sea salt and freshly ground black pepper

ROSEMARY TOAST SQUARES
3 slices bread, crusts removed and each cut into 9 squares
125 g butter, melted
1½ tablespoons finely chopped rosemary
a baking tray

ROSEMARY AÏOLI
180 ml good-quality mayonnaise
1 tablespoon crushed garlic
3 tablespoons finely chopped rosemary

Wrap the beef in clingfilm and place in the freezer for 2 hours. To make the Rosemary Toasts, preheat the oven to 180°C (350°F) Gas 4. Put the bread squares on a baking tray and brush with the melted butter mixture. Bake in the preheated oven for 10–15 minutes, until golden brown. To make the aïoli, put all the ingredients in a bowl and whisk to combine. Season to taste with salt and pepper. Remove the beef from the freezer, unwrap it and slice very thinly using a meat slicer or sharp knife. To assemble, put a small dollop of aïoli on a toast square, followed by a slice of beef. Drizzle with olive oil and season with salt and pepper.

Mini Lemon Millefeuilles
MAKES 30 MINI PASTRIES
125 g butter
1 teaspoon ground cinnamon
1 tablespoon sugar
450 g filo pastry dough, thawed if frozen
2 punnets fresh raspberries
400 ml whipping cream, whipped
icing sugar, to dust

For the lemon curd:
15 egg yolks
350 g sugar
180 ml freshly squeezed lemon juice
225 g cold butter, cut into cubes

To make the lemon curd, whisk together the egg yolks, sugar and lemon juice over a double boiler until thick and pale yellow, scraping the mixture down the sides of the bowl frequently. Remove from the heat and beat in the butter, one cube at a time. Refrigerate and leave to cool completely.

Preheat the oven to 180°C (350°F) Gas 4. Melt the butter and mix in the cinnamon and sugar. Lay one layer of filo on a baking tray and brush with the butter mixture. Continue to layer filo and butter for six layers. Put a second baking tray on top and bake in the preheated oven for 10–15 minutes or until golden brown. Leave to cool before cutting into 60 small squares (each one about 5 cm square.)

To assemble, lay out half the filo squares on a flat surface and spread with a little lemon curd. Arrange 4 raspberries on each square, add a dollop of cream and top with a second layer of filo. Dust with icing sugar and serve immediately.

A Birthday Cake Party

MENU FOR 8-10 GUESTS

APERITIF	French 75
FIRST COURSE TRIO	Wild Mushroom Bisque

Watercress, Baby Rocket and Mizuna Salad
With Walnut Vinaigrette, Toasted Walnuts and Edible Flowers

Filo Twists
With Wild Mushroom and Fontina Cheese Filling

MAIN COURSE   Asparagus Ravioli
With a Ricotta Cheese and Asparagus Filling

And a Topping of Baby Asparagus Tips, Broad Beans, Fresh Peas, Lemon Zest,

Orange Curls and Parmesan Cheese Curls

DESSERT   Chocolate Fudge Cake
With Chocolate Buttercream and Decorated with Chocolate Leaves

Surprise Party

At this party, the birthday cakes make it a real 'surprise party' for your guests because the cakes ARE the decoration. Although these cakes look good enough to eat they are made of flowers and are so fascinating that nobody would even think of cutting into one. We use a wide array of bright and happy floral colours to set the mood for fun. Our hanging 'chandeliers' are faux gift packages wrapped in contrasting colours and strung together from the crossbars of the arbour to hover amusingly over the table. Such an exceptional display as this calls for an equally unusual table covering so we gathered ribbons in similar festive colours and interlaced them into this fanciful top mixing solids, polka dots, stripes and chequered patterns with great abandon. This lighthearted and playful decoration matches the relaxed setting under this delightful backyard arbour and the delicate but satisfying menu.

above Each cake is a unique creation using roses, orchid petals, tropical flowers, carnations and leaves, with fresh fruit accents to produce an extraordinary cross between an actual birthday cake and a traditional floral centrepiece.

left Each place setting features an individual floral cupcake in its own fabric-wrapped box as a take-home memory of this fun day.

'Celebrations, congratulations, condolences, those occasions that involve the phrases 'I love you' and 'I'm sorry' – at every event and every moment in my life that requires flowers, Mark's Garden is in the picture. By now, the folks there know what we want and need, even better than we do. And we're talking about the last fifteen years! Simply put, Mark's Garden is part of my life.'

John Lithgow

French 75

MAKES 1 DRINK

30 ml gin
25 ml sugar syrup (page 73)
15 ml freshly squeezed lemon juice
chilled Champagne
lemon rind spiral for garnish
1 French sugar cube

Shake the first three ingredients well with
ice and strain into a chilled Champagne
glass. Top with Champagne and garnish
with lemon rind and a French sugar cube.

Wild Mushroom Bisque

MAKES 1.2 LITRES

700 g various wild mushrooms or button mushrooms
2 rashers streaky bacon, chopped
2 onions, chopped
2 cloves garlic, chopped
60 ml brandy
125 ml white wine
750 ml chicken stock
350 ml whipping cream
oil, for frying
sea salt and freshly ground black pepper

Clean the mushrooms with damp kitchen
paper or cloth and chop finely.

Put the bacon in a frying pan and sauté
over medium heat (without extra fat)
for 2–3 minutes. Add the onion, garlic
and mushrooms. Continue to sauté until
the mushrooms begin to brown. Add the
brandy and wine and simmer until most
of the liquid has evaporated. Add the
chicken stock and continue to simmer,
stirring occasionally, for 15 minutes.
Leave to cool.

Transfer the mixture to a blender in batches
and process until smooth. Pour into a large
bowl and stir in the cream. Season to taste
with salt and pepper. Cover the bowl or
transfer to a sealable container and
refrigerate until ready to use. Reheat gently
and serve.

Note: A few raw enoki mushrooms or slices
of sautéed mushrooms are a good topping.
Crumbled crisp-fried bacon and snipped
chives could also enhance the soup.

Watercress, Baby Rocket and Mizuna Salad

SERVES 8–10

250 g watercress
250 g baby rocket leaves
250 g mizuna
125 g toasted walnuts
edible flowers for garnish (optional)
sea salt and freshly ground pepper

For the Walnut Vinaigrette:
180 ml Champagne vinegar, plus extra to taste
2 tablespoons Dijon mustard
2 tablespoons brown sugar
1 tablespoon very finely chopped shallots
30 g toasted walnuts
180 ml walnut oil
60 ml olive oil

First make the Walnut Vinaigrette. Put all
the ingredients, except for the olive oil, in a
blender or food processor. Pulse to roughly
combine, then turn on. While the machine is
running, add the olive oil in a slow steady
stream to emulsify. Add seasoning to taste.

Put all the leaves in a large salad bowl and season with salt and pepper. Add the vinaigrette and toss well. Garnish with toasted walnuts and edible flowers, is using.

Filo Twists with Wild Mushroom and Fontina Cheese Filling
SERVES 8–10

8–10 sheets filo pastry dough, thawed if frozen
175 g butter, melted
8–10 aluminium ramekins or a cupcake tin

For the Wild Mushroom and Fontina Cheese Filling:
50 butter
2 shallots, very finely chopped
2 cloves garlic, crushed
450 g various wild mushrooms, chopped
1 tablespoon fresh thyme, finely chopped
1 tablespoon soy sauce
250 g cream cheese
125 g fontina cheese, grated
sea salt and freshly ground black pepper

To make the filling, melt the butter in a saucepan over medium heat and add the shallots and garlic. Sauté for 2–3 minutes. Add the mushrooms and thyme and continue to cook until the mushrooms have softened and begun to brown. Transfer the mushroom mixture to a bowl and add the soy sauce, cream cheese and fontina cheese. Mix well and season to taste with salt and pepper. Set aside until needed.

Preheat the oven to 190°C (375°F) Gas 5. Put a sheet of filo on a work surface and brush with melted butter. (Keep the remaining filo covered and moist with a damp cloth as you make the twists.) Fold the buttered filo in half and brush again with butter. Put a couple of tablespoons of the mushroom filling in the centre, gather the edges of the filo and twist. Brush with butter and put in an aluminium ramekin or cupcake tin. Repeat to make 8–10 twists. Place the ramekins on a baking tray and cook the twists in the preheated oven until golden brown, about 10 minutes.

Note: These twists may be prepared a few hours before serving, covered and chilled. When ready to serve, remove them from the ramekins or tin, put on an oiled baking tray and reheat in an oven preheated to 190°C (375°F) Gas 5 for 5 minutes.

Asparagus Ravioli
SERVES 8–10

For the Ricotta Cheese and Asparagus Filling:
175 g asparagus tips (reserve the stalks for the pasta), blanched and finely minced in a food processor
250 g ricotta cheese
75 g Parmesan cheese, freshly grated
⅛ teaspoon nutmeg
coarse salt and freshly ground black pepper
1 egg, beaten

For the pasta:
150 g asparagus stalks, blanched and finely minced
350 g plain flour, plus extra for sprinkling
1 teaspoon salt
3 eggs
a pasta machine (optional)

For the topping:
3 tablespoons olive oil
280 g baby asparagus tips, blanched
280 g broad beans, blanched
280 g fresh peas
zest of 3 unwaxed lemons
curls from 3 oranges
Parmesan cheese curls
sea salt and freshly ground black pepper

First make the filling. Place the blanched asparagus tips, ricotta, Parmesan and nutmeg in a mixing bowl. Combine well and season to taste with salt and pepper. Add the beaten egg and mix well.

To make the pasta, sift the flour and salt into food processor bowl and process with a metal blade. Add 1 of the eggs and pulse until mixed. Turn the processor to normal running and add the remaining eggs, one at a time, through the feeder tube. Continue processing until a dough is formed. Turn

the dough out onto a lightly floured surface. Shape the dough roughly into a ball and knead as you would bread, until it is smooth, pushing it away from you, then folding it back on itself. Give it a quarter turn and continue kneading, folding and turning for 5 minutes if you will be using a pasta machine, or for 10 minutes if you will be rolling it out by hand. The dough should be smooth and elastic. Wrap the dough in clingfilm and leave to rest for 15–20 minutes at room temperature. To roll out by hand: unwrap the dough and cut in half. Rewrap one half in clingfilm.

Lightly dust a clean work surface with flour. Put the unwrapped dough on the surface and lightly sprinkle with flour, flattening with the heel of your hand. Flip it and flatten again. With a floured rolling pin, roll the dough out and away from you, starting from the centre. Quarter turn the dough with each roll. Lightly flour if the dough gets too sticky. Continue until the dough is about

3 mm thick. Alternatively, use a pasta machine to roll out the pasta, following the manufacturer's instructions.

Cut the rolled dough into two lengths. With a spoon, evenly space 10–12 small mounds of ricotta cheese and asparagus filling on one side of one pasta strip. Lightly brush the pasta around each mound with water. Carefully fold the plain side of the pasta strip over the filling. Gently press around each mound, pushing any air out. Lightly dust with flour. Using a pasta wheel or knife, cut in between each mound to make semi-circles. Put the ravioli on a floured tea towel to dry. Repeat with the remaining dough.

When all the ravioli are made, drop them into a large pot of salted boiling water and boil for 4–5 minutes. Drain and transfer to a large bowl.

To make the topping, heat the olive oil in a large frying pan over medium/high heat. Sauté the vegetables until cooked, about 5 minutes. Season with salt and pepper. Lightly toss with the cooked ravioli. Arrange on a serving dish or individual dishes and garnish with lemon zest, orange curls and Parmesan cheese curls.

Note: An easy variation is to use wonton wrappers in place of pasta. Put a couple of tablespoons of asparagus filling on each wonton square and fold over into a triangle. Seal the edges with beaten egg. Poach in a shallow pan with a few centimetres of simmering water; the ravioli should take 3–4 minutes to cook. Drain and place on a platter. Top with the sautéed vegetables and other toppings as above. The wonton ravioli are very tender and best served warm.

Chocolate Fudge Cake with Chocolate Buttercream

SERVES 10-12

75 g bitter dark chocolate
260 g sifted plain flour, plus extra for flouring
2 teaspoons bicarbonate of soda
½ teaspoon salt
125 g butter, at room temperature, plus extra for greasing
500 g soft brown sugar
3 large eggs
1½ teaspoons vanilla extract
2 tablespoons Kahlúa or chocolate liqueur
250 ml soured cream
250 ml boiling water
1 quantity Chocolate Buttercream (see below)
Chocolate Leaves, to decorate (optional)
2 x 20-cm cake tins, greased and floured

For the Chocolate Buttercream:
175 g bitter dark chocolate, chopped
350 g dark chocolate, chopped
3 large egg whites, room temperature
250 g granulated sugar
⅛ teaspoon cream of tartar
½ teaspoon salt
450 g unsalted butter, room temperature
2 teaspoons vanilla extract
2 teaspoons instant espresso powder, dissolved in 1 teaspoon water
2 tablespoons dark rum

For the Chocolate Leaves:
250 g dark chocolate, chopped
16 lemon or camelia leaves, cleaned and dried

Preheat the oven to 180°C (350°F) Gas 4. Chop the chocolate and melt over low heat in a double boiler. Set aside.

Sift the flour, bicarbonate of soda and salt together in a separate bowl. Beat the butter in a large mixing bowl until softened. Gradually add the brown sugar and eggs to the butter. Continue beating until you have a smooth batter. Fold in the vanilla, Kahlúa and melted chocolate. Blend in the flour mixture a third at a time, then fold in the soured cream. Stir in the boiling water. Pour the batter into the prepared cake tins. Bake in

the preheated oven for 30 minutes or until the centre springs back when lightly pressed. Leave to cool slightly before tipping out on to cooling racks. Leave to cool completely before filling and frosting.

To make the Chocolate Buttercream put the two types of chocolate in a double boiler and stir until melted and smooth. Leave to cool. Mix the egg whites, sugar, cream of tartar and salt in the bowl of an electric mixer fitted with a whisk. Set the bowl over simmering water and heat the egg mixture until warm to the touch, about 5 minutes. Remove from the heat and whisk on high speed for 5 minutes until the mixture is cool and holds a stiff peak.

Add the butter, 1 tablespoon at a time, while whisking on medium speed. Scrape down the bowl, add the melted chocolate, vanilla, espresso and rum, and mix for 1 minute or until the chocolate is completely blended in. If the buttercream seems very soft, leave to cool and whisk it again.

To make the Chocolate Leaves, melt the chocolate in a double boiler. Remove from the heat and leave to cool slightly. Paint the melted chocolate onto the underside of a leaf using a butter knife or small paintbrush. Transfer, chocolate side up, to a baking sheet. Repeat with all the leaves and let them set. (They may be placed in the refrigerator for a few minutes to speed up the process.) When the chocolate has set firm, carefully pull away the leaves.

To assemble the cake, carefully slice each cooled cake round in half horizontally across the middle to create 4 cake rounds. Spread one-fifth of the buttercream on to one of the slices. Set a second layer on top. Spread one-fifth on the second layer and set a third layer on top. Spread one-fifth on the third layer and top with the last layer of cake. Use a palette knife to spread the rest of the buttercream evenly over the top and sides. Decorate with Chocolate Leaves, if using. Refrigerate until ready to serve.

A Fantasy Picnic

MENU FOR 6-8 GUESTS

APERITIF   Pineapple Mint Julep

DINNER   Spanish Almond Deviled Eggs
With Toasted Marcona Almonds

Crispy Fried Panko Chicken
With Fresh Peach Chutney

Green Beans and Asparagus
With Yellow Cherry Tomatoes and a Citrus Vinaigrette

Lambs' Lettuce, Rocket and Endive Salad
With a Champagne Vinaigrette

'The Kitchen's' Potato Salad
With Peas and Bacon

DESSERT   Apricot Oatmeal Bars

left Provence in the era of the French impressionists is the inspiration for this idealized picnic.

French Impressions

A private wooded road leading from our friend's home in Pasadena provides a perfect fantasy setting for a secluded 'country' picnic while remaining close to the city. We chose a fresh mixture of purple and golden tones, including sunflowers and lavender in willow baskets to evoke the mood of Provence and the great Impressionist painters. The dappled sunlight glistening through the trees reinforces that effect. However we move toward to a more sophisticated ambience than purely rustic by adding some vintage china, silver and crystal on a Battenberg lace tablecloth to complement our up-scaled lunch menu.

Rustic baskets packed with mixed varieties of sunflowers and cut lavender are set on the dining table and the picnic buffet. We placed tiny bouquets of cut lavender tied with a delicate lavender ribbon on each napkin and pinned sprigs to the lace tablecloth. We even gathered planted pots of coreopsis, blackeyed susan and Dutch iris around us to add more colour to the area, proving you can sometimes improve on nature by adding more nature! And if you look closely in the background, you can even see our prized handmade bench of birch branches for additional seating.

Pineapple Mint Julep

MAKES 1 DRINK

125 ml Maker's Mark bourbon (or other American whiskey)
60 ml mint syrup (see below)
30 ml fresh pineapple juice
sprigs of mint, to garnish
brown sugar swizzle stick, to serve (optional)

MINT SYRUP
450 g sugar
15–20 sprigs of mint

To make the Mint Syrup, put 450 ml water and the sugar in a saucepan over medium heat. Stir until the sugar has dissolved. Add the mint and simmer over low heat for 10 minutes. Remove from the heat and allow to cool, leaving the mint sprigs in the syrup. When completely cool, strain the syrup. Store in a sealable container in the refrigerator. It will keep for two weeks.

Fill a cocktail shaker with ice. Add all the ingredients and shake just to chill. Strain over crushed ice into a glass, such as an old-fashioned. Garnish with a large sprig of mint and add a brown sugar swizzle stick.

Spanish Almond Deviled Eggs

MAKES 16 PIECES

8 eggs
60 g butter
125 g Spanish Marcona almonds
60 g good-quality mayonnaise
1 tablespoon double cream or whole milk
½ teaspoon salt

Put the eggs in a saucepan and add cold water to cover. Bring just to the boil then remove from the heat. Cover the pan tightly, and let stand for 12–15 minutes. Drain the hot water from the pan and replace it with very cold water. Leave the eggs for 10 minutes.

Crack the eggs. Start at the largest end and, working under running water from the tap, gently remove the shells. Cut each egg in half lengthways. Remove the yolks and rub them through a fine mesh nylon sieve into a bowl.

Heat the butter in a heavy-based frying pan and sauté the almonds until golden brown. Remove the almonds from the pan using a slotted spoon. Stir the browned butter, mayonnaise, cream and salt into the egg yolks until well blended. Use a pastry bag or small spoon to fill the egg whites with the mixture. Top each filled egg with the almonds. Refrigerate until ready to serve.

above A colourful array of dishes makes an attractive display on the buffet table – the dappled sunlight enhancing the Mediterranean mood of this al fresco party.

Crispy Fried Panko Chicken

SERVES 8–10

60 g cornflour
60 g plain flour
125 g sugar
1½ teaspoons salt
2 eggs, lightly beaten
125 ml soy sauce
2 tablespoons finely grated fresh ginger
2 tablespoons finely chopped garlic
8–10 boneless chicken breasts or thighs
600 g Japanese Panko or other dry breadcrumbs
corn oil or vegetable oil, for frying

Combine all of the ingredients, except the chicken and breadcrumbs, in a large bowl. Mix until smooth. Add the chicken pieces, cover, and let marinate for several hours or overnight in the refrigerator.

Put the breadcrumbs on a baking tray. Roll the chicken pieces in the breadcrumbs to coat well. Pour the oil into a deep-fryer or fry in a large saucepan in 2.5 cm oil for about 15 minutes, turning frequently, until golden brown and cooked through. Drain on kitchen paper and cut into slices. Serve warm or cold, with Fresh Peach Chutney.

FRESH PEACH CHUTNEY

MAKES 1½ LITRES

900 g fresh peaches, diced (use frozen if fresh not available)
100 g mixed dried fruit such as cranberries, raisins, currants, sultanas and apricots
½ small red onion, finely chopped
125 g slivered almonds, toasted
125 ml cider vinegar
125 g sugar
a pinch of garam masala
a pinch of ground ginger
sea salt and freshly ground black pepper

Combine the fruits, onions and almonds in a large bowl and set aside. In a separate bowl, whisk together the vinegar, sugar and spices until well combined. Season to taste with salt and pepper. Pour the vinegar mixture over the fruit mixture and lightly toss to combine. Pour into sterilized jars and refrigerate for at least 2 days or until required. The mixture will keep for 1 month in the refrigerator.

Green Beans and Asparagus with Yellow Cherry Tomatoes

SERVES 8–10

450 g haricots verts, ends trimmed
900 g asparagus, tough ends trimmed
900 g yellow cherry tomatoes, cut in half
sea salt and freshly ground black pepper

CITRUS VINAIGRETTE

½ shallot, very finely chopped
250 ml extra virgin olive oil
125 ml freshly squeezed orange juice
60 ml freshly squeezed lemon juice
2 teaspoons caster sugar
1 teaspoon sea salt
½ teaspoon freshly ground black pepper

Bring a large pot of water to a simmer. Blanch the green beans and asparagus for 10 seconds or until just slightly tender and bright in colour. Remove from the pot and immediately submerge in a large bowl of ice water to stop the cooking process. Allow to cool completely, then drain. Set aside.

To make the vinaigrette, put all the ingredients into a bowl and whisk until well combined. To assemble the salad, place the green beans, asparagus and tomatoes in a

salad bowl and add the vinaigrette. Toss the ingredients together and adjust the seasoning. Transfer to a serving dish.

Lambs' Lettuce, Rocket and Endive Salad

SERVES 8-10

350 g large handfuls lambs' lettuce
350 g large handfuls wild rocket
3 chicory (Belgian endives), sliced into thick rings
a selection of edible flowers, to garnish (optional)

CHAMPAGNE VINAIGRETTE

250 ml good-quality olive oil
125 ml Champagne vinegar
freshly squeezed juice of ½ orange
1 teaspoon very finely chopped shallot
1 teaspoon caster sugar
a pinch of sea salt
a pinch of freshly ground black pepper

To make the vinaigrette, put the ingredients in a sealable container or jar and shake well. Adjust ingredients to taste; for example, if it is too sharp, add more oil or sugar.

To assemble the salad, put all the greens in a salad bowl, drizzle with the vinaigrette, and toss. Garnish with edible flowers, if desired.

'The Kitchen's' Potato Salad

SERVES 8-10

450 g-1 kg new potatoes, scrubbed but not peeled
6-8 bacon rashers, fried and chopped
400 g fresh or frozen peas, cooked
6 spring onions, thinly sliced

DRESSING

250 ml good-quality mayonnaise
250 ml sour cream
freshly squeezed juice of ½ lemon
1 tablespoon onion powder
1 tablespoon Dijon mustard
sea salt and freshly ground black pepper

Boil the potatoes until tender. While they are still warm, quarter or halve them, depending on size, and put in a large bowl. Stir in the bacon, peas and spring onions.

To make the dressing, put all the ingredients in a bowl, mix well and season to taste with salt and pepper. Toss the potato mixture in

the dressing and check the seasoning again if necessary. Transfer to a large serving platter.

Apricot Oatmeal Bars

MAKES 24 BARS

125 g sugar
450 g dried apricots, chopped plus extra to garnish
350 g melted butter
300 g brown sugar
1½ teaspoon bicarbonate of soda
175 g pecan nuts, chopped
280 g plain flour
280 g rolled oats

a 22 x 30 cm Swiss roll tin, lightly greased

Preheat the oven to 180°C (350°F) Gas 4. Put the sugar and dried apricots in a large saucepan with 125 ml water and cook until soft. Set aside.

In a bowl, combine the butter, sugar, bicarbonate of soda, pecans, flour and oatmeal. Take half of the mixture and press into the prepared Swiss roll tin. Spread the fruit evenly over the mixture. Sprinkle the remaining mixture on top of the fruit. Score with a sharp knife into squares or bars. Bake in the preheated oven for 25 minutes or until the top is golden brown. Allow to cool and cut into small squares or bars. Garnish with slices of dried apricot.

A Romantic Dinner for Two

MENU FOR 2

APERITIF	Rose Petal Martini
STARTER	Artichoke Soup with White Truffle Oil
	Served in an Artichoke Cup
MAIN COURSE	Beef Tournedo on an Asparagus Raft
	With a Red Wine Sauce and Crisp Root Vegetable Garnish
DESSERT	Boca Negra Cakes
	With Hot Fudge Sauce and White Chocolate Cream

True Romance

A gentleman is planning on proposing marriage tonight and he and his friends have gone to great lengths to make it as romantic and sexy an evening as possible. We have found a secluded balcony to allow our couple utmost privacy. By combining red and black we lend a contemporary 'gothic' tone to the décor, giving the setting an extra edge of sensuality. The secret, however, is that before placing the champagne to chill in a bucket nearby and lighting the candles on the table, we have hidden a ring box in the top of the floral centrepiece and covered it with roses. The lady may not be completely surprised by the proposal but she will be impressed with the gentleman's ingenuity.

Red roses, of course, are the historical symbol of romance and we are making the most of it. The centrepiece is a gorgeous grouping of mixed shades of red roses studded with and surrounded by glittering jewels for an added touch of glamour. A red striped rose is tucked into a rolled red silk napkin and more red roses 'rain' from the candlelit chandelier above the table. More red votive candles are nested in black quartz holders to provide a romantic glow and the setting is displayed on a sheer black organdy appliquéd tabletop placed over red silk.

Rose Petal Martini

MAKES 2 DRINKS

125 g granulated sugar
150 ml vodka
1 tablespoon freshly squeezed lemon juice
1–2 teaspoons ready-made rose syrup
fresh rose petals, to garnish

Make a sugar syrup by dissolving the sugar in 50 ml water in a saucepan over low heat. Bring to the boil then remove the pan from the heat and leave to cool completely.

Combine the vodka, lemon juice, rose syrup and 3 tablespoons of sugar syrup in a cocktail shaker filled with ice. Shake and strain into two well-chilled Martini glasses. Garnish with rose petals.

Artichoke Soup with White Truffle Oil

SERVES 8-10

5 artichokes
115 g butter
250 g shallots or white onion, finely chopped
1.75 litres chicken or vegetable stock
250 ml dry white wine
250 g potatoes, peeled and diced
250 ml double cream
white truffle oil, to taste
sea salt and freshly ground black pepper
vegetable or potato chips, to serve (optional)

For the steamed artichoke cups:
2 large globe artichokes
a bunch of thyme
sea salt and freshly ground black pepper

To make the artichoke cups, use a sharp knife to cut the top 1.5 cm from the artichokes and trim off the stems. Using scissors, cut the pointed edges off each leaf. Place the artichoke bottoms up in a steamer, adding the thyme, salt and pepper. Cover and cook for 30–40 minutes. When an outer leaf pulls away easily or a fork, is easily inserted in the centre, the artichoke is cooked. Drain the artichokes upside down until cool. Using a large spoon, hollow out the centre of each artichoke, so that it is large enough to fit a small cup. This is the cup in which the soup will be served. If necessary, trim the bottoms of each artichoke again, so that they will sit level on a plate. Set aside until needed.

To make the soup, cut the artichokes lengthways into quarters, and remove and discard the thistly chokes. Remove the leaves, leaving the artichoke hearts and 5 cm of stem. Chop into 1.5-cm pieces.

In a large saucepan, melt the butter and sauté the artichoke bottoms and shallots for about 5 minutes. Add the stock, wine and potatoes. Simmer until the potatoes and artichokes are tender. Let cool. Purée the soup in a blender or food mill, in batches if necessary. Refrigerate until ready to serve.

When ready to serve, reheat the liquid and whisk in the cream. Season to taste with salt, pepper and white truffle oil. Ladle into the prepared Artichoke Cups, garnish with a large vegetable or potato chip, and serve immediately. (Leftover soup can be poured into a sealable container and frozen.)

above Stylish and unusual presentation is key to impressive party food. Here, a simple artichoke soup has been served in a cup surrounded by a fresh artichoke, making an attractive serving dish.

Beef Tournedo on an Asparagus Raft

SERVES 2

800 g beef fillet, cleaned and trimmed
60 g butter
450 g asparagus spears, trimmed and steamed
sea salt and freshly ground black pepper

RED WINE SAUCE

MAKES 500 ML

1 bottle dry red wine (750 ml), plus extra to taste
1 litre beef stock
1 large onion, chopped
2 garlic cloves, crushed
1 carrot, chopped
1 tablespoon mustard powder
a few parsley sprigs
115 g cold butter, cubed
sea salt and freshly ground black pepper

CRISP ROOT VEGETABLE GARNISH (optional)

3–4 beetroots, carrots, onions or parsnips
corn oil, for deep frying
sea salt flakes

First make the red wine sauce. Combine the wine, stock, onion, garlic, carrot, mustard and parsley in a large saucepan. Bring to just below boiling and simmer until reduced to about 500 ml. Remove from the heat, strain and refrigerate. When ready to serve, reheat the sauce, whisking in the butter cube by cube until the sauce thickens. Season to taste with salt and pepper.

To make the crisp root vegetables, trim the tops and bottoms of the beetroots, carrots, onions or parsnips. Peel with a vegetable peeler and use a mandoline to slice them lengthways into long thin strips. Add about 15 cm of oil to a deep-fryer and heat to 180°C. Deep-fry the vegetables for about 2 minutes or until crisp. Drain them on kitchen paper and sprinkle with salt flakes.

To make the tournedos, slice the beef into 8–10 rounds. Save two rounds, and wrap and freeze the remaining beef for another time. Lightly pound the beef with a steak hammer and season with salt and pepper.

Melt 2 tablespoons butter in a heavy-based frying pan and sear the beef on each side. Transfer to a roasting tin. When ready to serve, finish in an oven preheated to 190°C (375°F) Gas 5 and roast for 8–12 minutes, until a thermometer inserted into the meat reads 46°C and the beef is still pink in the centre.

Sauté the asparagus spears in the remaining butter and season to taste. Arrange the asparagus in a 'raft' on two warmed serving plates. Put a beef round on top of each. Reheat the red wine sauce and spoon over the top. Garnish with crisp root vegetables, if using, and serve immediately.

Boca Negra Cakes

MAKES 12 SMALL CAKES

350 g good-quality dark chocolate, chopped
325 g sugar
125 ml bourbon
225 g unsalted butter, cut into 10 pieces
5 eggs, room temperature
1½ tablespoons plain flour
dark chocolate curls, to garnish

a 12-hole muffin tin, lightly greased
2 Martini glasses or glass serving dishes

HOT FUDGE SAUCE

115 ml double cream
40 g unsalted butter, cut into small pieces
75 g granulated sugar
75 g dark brown sugar, firmly packed
a pinch of salt
25 g sifted unsweetened cocoa powder

WHITE CHOCOLATE CREAM

(Note: this must be prepared 1 day in advance)
350 g white chocolate, finely chopped
250 ml double cream
60 ml bourbon, plus extra to taste
250 ml whipping cream, whipped to stiff peaks

To make the Hot Fudge Sauce, put the cream and butter in a heavy saucepan over medium heat. Stir until the butter is melted and the cream just comes to the boil. Add both sugars and stir for a few minutes until

they have dissolved. Reduce the heat. Add the salt and cocoa powder and whisk until smooth. Remove from the heat and transfer to a container with a tight-fitting lid. Refrigerate until ready to serve. Reheat in a metal bowl over simmering water, being careful not to let it scorch. (This sauce will keep for 2–3 weeks in the refrigerator.)

To make the White Chocolate Cream, put the white chocolate in the bowl of a food processor fitted with a metal blade, or into a blender. Heat the double cream in a small saucepan over medium heat until small bubbles form around the edge of the pan. Pour the cream over the chocolate and blend until completely smooth. Add the bourbon, taste and add more, if desired. Transfer to a container with a tight-fitting lid and chill overnight. When ready to serve, bring the mixture to room temperature and gradually fold in the whipped cream.

To make the cakes, preheat the oven to 180°C (350°F) Gas 4. Put the chopped chocolate in a medium bowl. In a large saucepan, mix 225 g of the sugar and the bourbon and cook over medium heat, stirring occasionally, until the sugar dissolves and the mixture comes to the boil. Immediately pour the hot syrup over the chocolate and stir with a wooden spoon, beating in the butter one piece at a time, until well blended.

Beat the eggs until pale yellow. Gradually add the flour to the eggs. Slowly pour the chocolate mixture into the egg mixture, beating constantly. Pour the cake batter into the prepared muffin tin. Bake in the preheated oven for 20–25 minutes. Leave to cool for 5 minutes, then turn out onto a wire rack. Note: once cool, the extra cakes can be frozen and enjoyed another time.

To serve, pour 2 tablespoons reheated Hot Fudge Sauce into each serving glass. Carefully place a cake on top. Top with White Chocolate Cream and garnish with chocolate curls. Serve immediately.

Christmas Nouveau

MENU FOR 8–10

APERITIF	Garnet Slip
TO BE PASSED	Caviar and Smoked Salmon Blini Puffs With Crème Fraîche and Lemon Zest
BUFFET	Celeriac Salad With a Dijon Vinaigrette
	Braised Brussels Sprouts With Pistachio Nuts
	Festive Rice With Leeks, Marcona Almonds and Morello Cherries
	Pork Roast with Cumberland Sauce With an Apricot, Prune and Cranberry Stuffing
	Lobster Thermidor Served on a Bed of Rock Salt
	Roasted Cornish Game Hens With Sage Sausage and Mushroom Stuffing
DESSERT	Bavarian Cream

A Feast for the Eyes

Christmas entertaining is generally about maintaining tradition, but we like to create some new traditions too. Our buffet table in this comfortable California Craftsman home is laden with classic foods with our own variations and some complete surprises like Lobster Thermidor. By the same token, our décor is a new take on the old standbys. We have chosen a deep rich red palette to denote the season and complement the warmth of the dark wood panelling and furniture as well as the colourful displays of food. Antique silver pieces display innovative Christmas trees and 'ornaments' that are made of fresh flowers, of course, and fresh fruit.

Our Christmas trees are oversized cones of pavéd large bloom red roses with ornate toppers. Instead of placing traditional ornaments on the trees, we have made some out of flowers and set them on silver pedestals and candle stands. In addition to roses, we have pavéd our Christmas trees and ornamental balls with cherries and raspberries. The red silk napkins are tied with silver tassels to add some sparkle. Tall taper candles mixed with fat pillar candles add a further touch of warmth and hospitality. The overall effect is a feast for the eyes as well as the palate. Eat, drink and be merry.

Garnet Slip

MAKES 1 DRINK

30 ml vodka
15 ml limoncello (Italian lemon liqueur)
60–90 ml fresh raspberry juice
60–90 ml fresh or tinned peach juice or nectar
fresh lemon zest and fresh raspberries, to garnish
a Martini glass rimmed with caster sugar

Put the vodka, limoncello and juices in a
cocktail shaker and mix well with cracked
ice. Strain into a glass. Garnish with lemon
zest and raspberries. Serve immediately.

Caviar and Smoked Salmon Blini Puffs

MAKES 24 PUFFS

450 g cottage cheese
1 tablespoon soured cream
1 teaspoon vanilla extract
½ teaspoon sugar
3 tablespoons butter, melted
3 eggs
60 g plain flour
250 ml crème fraîche
120 g caviar and/or smoked salmon
zest from 1 unwaxed lemon, to garnish
2 x 12-hole cupcake tins, greased

Preheat the oven to 180°C (350°F) Gas 4.
Put the first 7 ingredients in a food
processor and blend until smooth. Pour
the batter into the prepared cupcake tins
and bake in the preheated oven for
12–15 minutes or until golden brown.

To assemble, spoon a small amount of
crème fraîche onto each blini, then top with
a slice of smoked salmon or small amount of
caviar. Garnish with lemon zest.

Note: the puffs may be made ahead of time,
frozen, and reheated at 180°C (350°F)
Gas 4. The Kitchen has found that the blinis
are delicious when they are reheated in a
deep-fat fryer.

Celeriac Salad

SERVES 8

2 large celeriac, trimmed and peeled
2–3 carrots, cleaned and trimmed
butterhead lettuce leaves, to serve

DIJON VINAIGRETTE
60 ml white balsamic vinegar
½ teaspoon salt
2 tablespoons Dijon mustard
180 ml extra virgin olive oil
2 tablespoons very finely chopped shallots
1 tablespoon black pepper

To make the Dijon Vinaigrette, mix the
vinegar, salt and mustard in a food
processor. Slowly add the oil in a steady
stream until an emulsion forms. Add the
shallots and pepper. Quarter the celeriac.
In a food processor, shred them and the
carrots with a coarse grating disc. Add the
vinaigrette, toss the salad and serve on
a bed of butterhead lettuce leaves.

Braised Brussels Sprouts

SERVES 8–10

900 g fresh, leafy Brussels sprouts
2–3 tablespoons butter or extra virgin olive oil
2 tablespoons very finely chopped shallots
60 ml chicken or vegetable stock
60 g pistachio nuts, shelled
salt and freshly ground black pepper

Peel the sprouts as far as possible, reserving
the leaves. Shred the cores. Melt the butter
in a large frying pan, add the shallots and
sauté for 2–3 minutes. Add the Brussels
sprout leaves and shredded cores and sauté
for another minute or two. Add the stock and
simmer until the sprouts are tender. Season
to taste and top with pistachios.

Festive Rice
SERVES 8

450 g basmati rice
4 cardamom pods
6 small leeks, white and light green part only, sliced
1 tablespoon olive oil or butter
125 g Spanish Marcona almonds
125 g tinned or jarred morello cherries, drained
salt and freshly ground black pepper

Wash and drain the rice. Bring 700 ml water to a rolling boil. Stir in the rice and a pinch of salt. Return to the boil. Add the cardamom, cover and reduce the heat. Simmer for 15 minutes. Remove from heat and keep covered for 15 minutes. Sauté the leeks in olive oil until soft. Add the almonds and sauté, adding the cherries last. When hot, add to the rice, season to taste and serve.

Pork Roast with Cumberland Sauce
SERVES 8-10

2.7-3.5 kg pork loin roast, bone in
150 g dried cranberries
150 g dried prunes, chopped
150 g dried apricots, chopped
1 apple, cored and chopped
300 ml Calvados (French apple brandy)
50 g unsalted butter
2 large onions, finely chopped
salt and freshly ground black pepper

CUMBERLAND SAUCE
75 ml port
150 ml freshly squeezed orange juice
1½ tablespoons freshly squeezed lemon juice
60 ml redcurrant jelly
¼ teaspoon ground ginger
¼ teaspoon salt
2 tablespoons cornflour and 2 tablespoons water
30 g unsalted butter

Preheat the oven to 190°C (375°F) Gas 5. Using a knife, make a 3–5-cm hole through the centre of the loin; set aside. Combine the fruit and Calvados in a bowl and leave to macerate for an hour. Melt the butter in a frying pan. Add the onion and sauté until tender and slightly caramelized. Add the onion and any juices to the fruit, then drain, saving the liquid. Stuff the fruit into the pork, baste with the reserved marinade and season. Put the pork on a rack and roast in the preheated oven for 1½ hours or until a thermometer inserted into the meat reads 65.5°C. Leave the pork to rest for 15 minutes while you make the sauce.

To make the Cumberland Sauce, skim all but 1 tablespoon fat from the roasting tin. Put the tin across two burners, add 125 ml water and boil over high heat to deglaze. Scrape up any brown bits. Add the port and boil for 1 minute. Add the orange and lemon juices, jelly, ginger and salt and whisk until the jelly is dissolved. Whisk together the cornflour and water in a cup, then add to the tin and simmer, whisking, until the sauce is thickened, about 1 minute. Remove from the heat and whisk in the butter. Pour through a sieve and serve hot.

Lobster Thermidor
SERVES 8

250 g butter, melted
freshly squeezed juice of 1 lemon
2 tablespoons each of chives and dill, snipped
8-10 lobster tails, meat removed and shells saved

For the sauce:
60 g unsalted butter
1 onion, finely chopped
2 tablespoons plain flour
60 ml dry sherry or white wine
250 ml whipping cream
1 tablespoon paprika
2 tablespoons tomato purée
sea salt and freshly ground black pepper
rock salt, to display (optional)

Preheat the oven to 170°C (325°F) Gas 3. Combine the butter, lemon juice, chives and dill. Brush the lobster meat with the butter mixture. Place it in a roasting tin with the lobster shells. Roast in the preheated oven for 25–30 minutes, until the meat is opaque. Remove from the oven, put 1 tablespoon of the remaining butter mixture in the bottom of each shell. Cut the meat crossways into pieces and return it to the shells. Melt the butter in a frying pan, add the onion and sauté until softened. Add the flour and cook, stirring, until golden brown. Add the sherry, cream, paprika and tomato purée. Cook until the mixture thickens and season to taste. Arrange the lobster tails over rock salt, ladle over the sauce and serve immediately.

Roasted Cornish Game Hens
SERVES 8

8 Cornish game hens, boned
2 tablespoons butter or extra virgin olive oil
2 large onions, chopped
900 g sage-flavoured sausagemeat
675 g mushrooms, sliced
4 tablespoons chopped parsley
sea salt and freshly ground black pepper
wooden skewers

Preheat the oven to 180°C (350°F) Gas 4. Rinse the Cornish game hens and season well. Melt the butter in a frying pan and sauté the onions until tender. Add the sausagemeat, sauté until no longer pink then add the mushrooms and sauté for 2–3 minutes. Add the parsley and drain off any remaining liquid. Fill each Cornish hen with about 250 g stuffing and secure with skewers. Chill until ready to cook. Roast in the preheated oven for 50–60 minutes or until a thermometer inserted into the meat reads 74°C. Remove the skewers and serve.

Bavarian Cream
SERVES 8-10

3 tablespoons unflavoured powdered gelatine
6 egg yolks
250 g granulated sugar
500 ml milk
1 tablespoon vanilla extract
60 ml brandy or other liqueur of your choice
500 ml whipping cream, whipped
fresh cranberries or other red berries, to garnish
1 large decorative mould

Soak the gelatine in 150 ml water for about 5 minutes, or until it has softened and swelled. Whisk the egg yolks in a bowl and gradually add the sugar. Continue to whisk until the mixture is pale yellow. In a saucepan, bring the milk to a full simmer. Remove from the heat and slowly pour into the yolks, whisking constantly. Put the egg and milk in a double boiler. Whisk until the mixture thickens and coats the back of a spoon. Add the gelatine, vanilla and brandy, and beat well. Put the bowl over a larger bowl of iced water. Stir continuously until the mixture is cool and continues to thicken. Gently fold in the whipped cream using a spatula. Pour into the mould and chill overnight before serving.

A Whimsical New Year's Eve

MENU FOR 8-10 GUESTS

APERITIF Elderflower Champagne Cocktail
With Edible Gold Leaf and Miniature Gardenia Garnish

STARTER Caviar Bar
Caviar of your Choice and Smoked Salmon

A Selection of Trimmings

Served with Wild Rice Blinis, Blini Puffs and Toast Points

FIRST COURSE Crab and Lobster Bisque with Sherry
Garnished with Mini Puff Pastry Stars

SECOND COURSE Ruby Salad
With a Pomegranate Vinaigrette

THIRD COURSE Miniature Penne with Black Truffle Sage Cream Sauce
With Parmesan Cheese Curls and Fried Sage Leaves

FOURTH COURSE Lollipop Lamb Chops
With a Pomegranate Wine Sauce and Fresh Mint Relish

FIFTH COURSE Chocolate Mousse Shooters

Midnight Watch

One of the cardinal rules of New Year's Eve is to have a good time and that is what we kept in mind in designing this wacky assemblage sculpture to keep track of the countdown to midnight at this party. We include plenty of clocks to view from any angle in the room and not let anyone lose track of time. Our intent is to keep things high-spirited and fun, in line with the objective of the party. That means lots of colour and lots of movement and we selected the energetic combination of turquoise and coral as a starting point.

This celebration is in the fanciful living room of the former Tony Duquette estate in Beverly Hills, which inspired us to reflect the fantastical designs that he frequently created for the stage and screen in the mid-twentieth century. In the pursuit of an extravagantly theatrical display we wanted a tall piece to make as dramatic a statement as possible –

something in which Duquette specialized. We had fun putting together an unusual pastiche of flowers including eremerus, protea, cock's comb, roses, button mums, freesia, dendrobium orchids, dahlias and zinnias. We combined them with swirls of conch shells, star fish that we painted turquoise, cascades of clam shells and a variety of found trinkets and fabric pieces mirroring some of the unusual undersea elements in the house's extraordinary interior.

As a bizarre touch we even painted bronze 'hands of time' to reach out from behind the impressive floral sculpture to welcome the guests. Turquoise taper candles highlight this display as well as candelabras placed throughout the party area. A caviar bar stands nearby, capturing the same spirit of decadence, and an exquisite five-course tasting menu is served throughout the long evening.

Elderflower Champagne Cocktail

MAKES 10 DRINKS

10 tablespoons elderflower cordial
2 bottles Champagne, chilled
edible gold leaf
10 miniature white gardenias or rose petals
10 bolla or large wine glasses, chilled

Place 1 tablespoon elderflower cordial in each glass. Top up with chilled Champagne. Sprinkle edible gold leaf on top of each drink and float a miniature gardenia or rose petals to garnish. Serve immediately.

Note: The edible gold leaf is available at specialist kitchen shops and online.

Caviar Bar

SERVES 8-10

2–3 varieties of caviar of your choice
    (allow about 50 g per person)
1 bunch chives, snipped
1 small mild onion, very finely chopped
250 ml crème fraîche or soured cream
2–3 ripe avocados, peeled, stoned and chopped
freshly grated zest from 2 unwaxed lemons
90 g capers in brine, drained
24 wild rice blinis or Blini Puffs (see page 81)
24 toast points (6 slices of toasted bread,
    crusts removed and sliced into quarters)
a selection of prepared unsalted crackers
1 side of smoked salmon, sliced
3–4 fillets of smoked trout
8–10 decorative caviar spoons

Keep the caviar in its tins and find an attractive platter for the smoked fish. Arrange the other ingredients in Martini glasses, Champagne coupes and glass or silver icers. Fill a large, decorative silver or glass container with plenty of ice. Arrange the caviar and trimmings on top of the ice. Heat the blinis and keep them warm by wrapping them in a starched linen napkin. Be sure to use caviar spoons.

Note: Often, inexpensive caviar spoons are found in second-hand stores, Asian markets or festive catalogues. At The Kitchen, we pass caviar, crème fraîche and lemon zest on these spoons as an easy passed starter.

Crab and Lobster Bisque with Mini Puff Pastry Stars

SERVES 8–10

175 g butter
1 large onion, finely chopped
2 large shallots, very finely chopped
40 g flour
500 ml single cream
500 ml fish, vegetable or chicken stock
500 ml double cream
125 ml dry sherry or white wine
1 teaspoon Tabasco sauce or other hot sauce
1 tablespoon paprika
450 g well-cleaned crab meat
225 g well-cleaned lobster meat, chopped

Mini Puff Pastry Stars:
1 sheet ready-made puff pastry dough, thawed
60 ml milk
a small star-shaped cutter
a baking tray, lightly greased

In a medium stockpot over medium/low heat, melt 125 g butter and sauté the onion and shallots for 5 minutes. Stir in the flour and cook for another few minutes. Gradually add the single cream, fish stock, double cream and sherry and continue cooking until slightly thickened. Season to taste with salt, pepper, Tabasco sauce and paprika.

Melt the remaining butter in a frying pan over medium heat. Add the crab and lobster meat and sauté until heated through. Add to the soup and season to taste. When cool, purée the soup in a blender.

Preheat the oven to 180°C (350°F) Gas 4. Lay the puff pastry out on a flat surface. Cut out several stars and place on the prepared baking tray. Lightly brush with milk. Bake in the preheated oven for 10–12 minutes or until golden. When ready to serve, gently reheat the soup, ladle into serving bowls, and garnish with pastry stars.

Ruby Salad with Pomegranate Vinaigrette

SERVES 8–10

4–5 heads baby red leaf lettuce, torn
2 heads radicchio, cored and torn
3–4 heads red chicory, sliced lengthways
75 g dried cranberries
75 g dried cherries
3 red beetroots, roasted, peeled and sliced lengthways
75 g pomegranate seeds
125 g candied or toasted pecans
350 g St. Agur (blue cheese), crumbled
sea salt and freshly ground black pepper

For the Pomegranate Vinaigrette:
60 ml pomegranate juice
60 ml white balsamic vinegar
1 shallot, very finely chopped
1 tablespoon chopped mint
1 tablespoon pomegranate molasses
180 ml rapeseed oil or extra virgin olive oil
sea salt and freshly ground black pepper

To make the Pomegranate Vinaigrette, put the pomegranate juice, vinegar, shallot, mint and pomegranate molasses in a bowl and whisk to combine. Gradually whisk in the oil. Season to taste with salt and pepper and set aside until needed.

Put the salad leaves in a bowl and toss to mix. Add all the remaining salad ingredients. Season with salt and pepper. Add a few tablespoons of the Pomegranate Vinaigrette and toss well. Add a little more, if needed.

Note: Alternatively you could put the dressed salad leaves on a platter and arrange the remaining ingredients around the outside edge, to form a garland.

Miniature Penne with Black Truffle Sage Cream Sauce

SERVES 8-10

450 g mini-penne pasta
2 tablespoons unsalted butter
75 g shallots, very finely chopped
3 tablespoons chopped sage
500 ml dry white wine
750 ml double cream
black truffle oil, to taste
16–20 sage leaves
corn or vegetable oil, for frying
sea salt and freshly ground black pepper
Parmesan cheese curls, to serve

Bring a large pot of water to a full boil, add
a couple dashes of salt and the pasta. Cook
until the pasta is just tender. Drain, rinse,
return to the pan and cover to keep warm.

Melt the butter in a saucepan over medium
heat. Add the shallots and sage. Sauté for
about 30 seconds. Whisk in the wine and
cream. Increase the heat and bring to a
soft boil until the sauce is reduced and
thickened. Add black truffle oil to taste,

starting with about 1 tablespoon. Season to
taste with salt and pepper. Pour the sauce
over the pasta and mix. Adjust the seasoning
and truffle oil again, if needed. Heat about
5 cm of oil in a large frying pan or wok. Fry
the sage leaves until crisp and drain on
kitchen paper. Spoon the pasta into bowls
and garnish with sage leaves and Parmesan.

Lollipop Lamb Chops

MAKES 24 CHOPS

3 tablespoons each chopped fresh rosemary,
    mint and basil
olive oil, for brushing
3–8 rib racks of lamb, well trimmed and frenched
sea salt and freshly ground black pepper
Pomegranate Wine Sauce and Fresh Mint Relish,
    to serve (see below)

a rimmed baking tray

Put the herbs in a small bowl and mix
together. Brush the lamb with oil and season
with salt and pepper. Sprinkle the herb
mixture over the lamb. Put in the refrigerator
and marinate for an hour or longer.

Preheat the oven to 240°C (475°F) Gas 9.
Place the racks on a rimmed baking tray and
roast for about 10 minutes or until a meat
thermometer inserted into the centre reads
54°C. Cut between the bones to make
individual chops. Serve with Pomegranate
Wine Sauce and Fresh Mint Relish.

POMEGRANATE WINE SAUCE

MAKES 750 ML

1 onion, finely chopped
60 g butter
500 ml pomegranate juice
250 ml red wine
250 ml beef stock
1 sprig rosemary
60 ml pomegranate molasses
2 tablespoons cornflour, dissolved in 60 ml water
sea salt and freshly ground black pepper

Sauté the onion in a frying pan with the
butter until softened. Add the pomegranate
juice, red wine, beef stock, rosemary and
bring to the boil. Lower the heat and leave
to simmer for several minutes.

Keep the pan over heat and whisk in the
cornflour and water mixture. When the sauce
has thickened, add the pomegranate

molasses and salt and pepper to taste.
Strain the sauce, transfer to a resealable
container and refrigerate for up to 2 days.
Reheat to serve.

FRESH MINT RELISH

MAKES 250 ML

125 g each mint leaves and flat leaf parsley
16 cornichons, cut in half
4 teaspoons capers
125 ml extra virgin olive oil
4 teaspoons white wine vinegar, or to taste
2 tablespoons granulated sugar
sea salt and freshly ground black pepper

Put the mint and parsley leaves in a food
processor and blend until finely chopped.
Scrape down the sides. Add the cornichons
and capers and process to combine. With
the motor running, pour the oil down the
funnel. Add the vinegar and sugar, and
season well with salt and pepper. Transfer
to a resealable container and refrigerate
until ready to use. The sauce will keep for
up to 1 week.

Chocolate Mousse Shooters

MAKES 20 SHOOTERS

250 g dark chocolate, roughly chopped
3 tablespoons Kahlúa or liqueur of your choice
1 tablespoon vanilla extract
125 g unsalted butter, cut into cubes
8 large egg yolks
125 g granulated sugar
5 egg whites
250 ml double cream, whipped

Melt the chocolate, liqueur and vanilla
extract in a double boiler, stirring
continuously. Remove from the heat and
gradually whisk in the butter. Combine the
egg yolks and sugar in a mixing bowl and
whisk until thick and pale yellow. Slowly
add the chocolate mixture and blend well.
Beat the egg whites until soft peaks form.
Gently fold the egg whites, ¼ at a time, into
the chocolate and egg yolk mixture.

Chill until ready to serve. Just before serving,
fold in the whipped cream. Spoon into small
shot or aperitif glasses to serve.

Chinese New Year

MENU FOR 8–10 GUESTS

APERITIF   Lychee Collins

BUFFET   Crab Salad Lettuce Cups

Watercress and Mizuna Tropical Fruit Salad
With a Miso Vinaigrette

Stir-Fried Chinese Vegetables

Braised Short Ribs
With Chinese Barbecue Sauce

Prawn and Sweetcorn Fritters

Langoustine and Papaya
Served on Sugar Cane Skewers and with Sweet Chilli Sauce

DESSERT   Individual Pear Tatins

Sesame Seed Tuiles

Fortune Cookies
Dipped in Chocolate and Sprinkled with Gold Dust

Gold Rush

In Chinese tradition, decorating the home on New Year's Day in red and gold brings happiness and wealth. Our grand celebration in the style of Chinese New Year uses gold upon gold upon gold to create a unique and lustrous tabletop that casts a burnished glow and mesmerizes guests into a mood of well-being and celebration. The table linen of gold silk is overlaid with a sheer top cloth decorated with gold appliqué. Gold chargers with gold-rimmed plates and glasses and gold cutlery create an exciting and sumptuous look accented by the warmth of gold-leafed tea-light holders spread around the table.

Chinese vase stands have been painted gold and stacked high on the table to resemble a pagoda. Broad-leaved succulent plants have been painted gold and tucked into its base. Gold-painted bamboo is inserted horizontally and balanced by red lanterns as explosive sprays of yellow oncidium orchids and gold-coloured cymbidium orchids spill from the top.

far right As a final touch, red napkins tied with prosperity bracelets rest against traditional individualized name stamps, selected for each guest as their place card.

Lychee Collins

MAKES 1 DRINK

75 ml gin

4 tablespoons freshly squeezed lemon or lime juice

2 tablespoons sugar syrup (see page 73)

2 tablespoons liquid from tinned lychees

soda water

lychee or edible flower, to garnish

Pour the first 4 ingredients into a cocktail shaker filled with ice. Fill a highball glass with crushed ice and strain the drink from the shaker into the glass. Top up with soda water. Garnish and serve immediately.

Crab Salad Lettuce Cups

SERVES 8–10

750 g cooked crabmeat, picked over for cartilage

3 medium tomatoes, peeled, deseeded and chopped

2 small cucumbers, chopped

2 tablespoons finely chopped mint

2 tablespoons chopped chives

2 tablespoons chopped coriander

1 tablespoon freshly grated lemon zest

125 ml rice wine vinegar or sherry vinegar

2 tablespoons soy sauce

175 ml olive or rapeseed oil

iceberg or butterhead lettuce, to serve

coriander sprigs, to garnish

salt and freshly ground black pepper

Combine the crab, tomatoes, cucumbers, mint, chives and coriander in a bowl. In a separate small bowl, mix the lemon zest, rice wine vinegar and soy sauce. Whisk in the olive oil and season to taste with salt and pepper. Prepare the lettuce cups using the inner leaves only. To serve, dress the salad with the vinaigrette and fill the lettuce cups. Garnish with coriander sprigs and serve immediately.

Watercress and Mizuna Tropical Fruit Salad

SERVES 8–10

2 bunches watercress, long stems trimmed

250 g mizuna

2 tablespoons white miso paste

1 teaspoon prepared wasabi

2 tablespoons rice wine vinegar

75 ml rapeseed or olive oil

1 pineapple, peeled, cored and cut lengthways into 5–7.5-cm slices

2 mangos, peeled, stoned and sliced crossways into 5–7.5 cm slices

½ medium daikon, peeled and coarsely grated

sea salt and freshly ground pepper

Put the leaves in a salad bowl. In a separate small bowl, combine the miso, wasabi and rice wine vinegar. Whisk in the oil and season to taste with salt and pepper. Pour sufficient vinaigrette over the greens to moisten. Arrange the pineapple, mango and daikon on top. Serve immediately.

Stir-fried Chinese Vegetables

SERVES 8–10

50 ml corn or vegetable oil

1 onion, cut into 5-mm wedges

2 tablespoons grated fresh ginger

3 garlic cloves, crushed

1 teaspoon dried chilli flakes

2 red peppers, cut into vertical slices

2 yellow peppers, cut into vertical slices

250 g sugar snap peas, trimmed

250 g mangetout, trimmed

250 g frozen edamame, defrosted

1 bunch baby red radishes, cleaned and cut in half

6 baby pak-choi, cut in half

50 ml bottled spicy Thai sauce

Heat a wok over high heat until a bead of water evaporates on contact. Pour in the oil and reduce the heat to medium. Add the onions and toss until slightly soft. Add the ginger, garlic, chilli flakes and peppers and toss until the peppers have softened, about 2 minutes. Add the sugar snap peas, mangetout, edamame, radishes and baby pak-choi and toss until hot, about 3 minutes. Add the spicy Thai sauce, toss and serve immediately.

Braised Short Ribs with Chinese Barbecue Sauce

SERVES 8–10

2.7 kg pork short ribs, boned

50 ml oil

6 garlic cloves, peeled and crushed

2 onions, peeled and chopped

450 ml bottled barbecue sauce

a 5–7.5-cm piece fresh ginger, peeled and grated

salt and freshly ground black pepper

a large roasting tin

Preheat the oven to 230°C (450°F) Gas 8. Put the ribs in a large roasting tin with 450 ml water and season. Roast in the preheated oven for 25 minutes. Remove from the oven, turn the ribs over and return them to the oven to roast for 25 minutes more. Remove them from the oven a second time and reserve any meat juices from the tin. Reduce the oven temperature to 190°C (375°F) Gas 5. Heat the oil in a frying pan and fry the garlic and onions until softened. Add the reserved meat juices, barbecue sauce and ginger and heat through. Pour the mixture over the ribs, cover with foil and roast for about 2 hours or until the ribs are tender.

Taste to check the seasoning and consistency. Add salt and pepper if necessary and if the batter is too thin, add a few tablespoons of flour. Working in batches, drop tablespoons of batter into the oil and fry each until golden brown. Remove from the pan with a slotted spoon and drain on kitchen towels. Serve immediately.

Langoustine and Papaya on Sugar Cane Skewers
MAKES 24–30 SKEWERS
2 x 250–300-g langoustine tails, cooked
1–2 papayas or mangos, peeled and seeded/stoned
bottled Thai sweet chilli sauce, to serve
24–30 sugar cane sticks or bamboo skewers

Clean and slice the langoustine tails into 5 mm thick slices. Thinly slice the papaya lengthways. Weave slices of papaya and langoustine onto the sugar cane sticks, alternating the two. Chill and brush with Thai sweet chilli sauce before serving.

Individual Pear Tatins
SERVES 8–10
350 g sugar
125 ml water
2 tablespoons pear liqueur or Grand Marnier
8–10 Comice pears
250 g butter, melted
450 g ready-made puff pastry, thawed if frozen
8–10 ramekins or foil cups

Preheat the oven to 190°C (375°F) Gas 5. Combine the sugar, water and liqueur in a saucepan and heat until they caramelize. Pour some of the caramel into the ramekins or foil cups. Let rest while you peel and core the pears. Trim them by cutting off the top and bottom so they will sit in the ramekins without wobbling. Put each one in a ramekin and brush with melted butter. Put on a baking tray and bake in the preheated oven for 30–35 minutes, until just tender.

Roll out the puff pastry on a lightly floured surface and cut into circles to fit the ramekins. Remove the pears from the oven and put a puff pastry round on top of each ramekin. Return to the oven and bake for another 20–25 minutes or until the fruit is soft and the puff pastry browned. When cool

Prawn and Sweetcorn Fritters
MAKES 12–36 FRITTERS
50 g plain flour
½ teaspoon baking powder
½ teaspoon salt
1 large egg, beaten
3 tablespoons coconut milk or milk
1 teaspoon grated fresh ginger
1 teaspoon hot sauce or dried chilli flakes
280 g fresh sweetcorn kernels
125 g uncooked prawns, finely chopped
75 g spring onion, chopped
rapeseed or vegetable oil, for frying
sea salt and freshly ground black pepper

Sift together the flour, baking powder and salt. Put the egg, coconut milk, ginger and hot sauce in a bowl and mix. Add the flour mixture and stir until just combined. Add the sweetcorn, prawns and spring onion and gently stir to mix.

When ready to serve, heat a few inches of oil in a wok or deep-fryer. Drop 1 tablespoon of batter into the oil and fry until golden.

enough to handle, carefully turn the tatins out onto serving plates and drizzle with the remaining caramel sauce. Serve immediately, or reheat before serving.

Sesame Seed Tuiles
MAKES 12 LARGE OR 24 SMALL TUILES
175 g icing sugar
125 g butter, softened
175 g toasted sesame seeds
50 g plain flour
125 ml freshly squeezed orange juice or milk
1 tablespoon finely grated orange zest
a baking tray, greased and lined with
    parchment paper or a silicone baking mat

Preheat the oven to 170°C (325°F) Gas 3. Combine all the ingredients in a mixing bowl and beat well. Put 1 tablespoon batter for a small tuile, or 2 tablespoons batter for a large tuile, on the prepared baking tray. Spread out very thinly using a spatula. Bake in the preheated oven for 5–8 minutes or until golden. Working quickly, lift the tuiles one at a time and roll them around a narrow rolling pin or wood dowel. Slide off the tip of the rolling pin and put on a plate to cool. If any tuiles harden before you roll them, return to the oven for 1 minute to soften.

Store the tuiles in a large airtight container and use within 1 week of making.

Chocolate and Gold Fortune Cookies
MAKES 16 COOKIES
16 purchased Chinese fortune cookies
140 g dark chocolate
edible gold dust, to decorate

Melt the chocolate in a metal bowl over simmering water, being careful not to scorch it. Stir with a rubber spatula until completely melted and smooth.

Let the chocolate cool slightly then, holding a cookie firmly, dip its bottom half into the melted chocolate. Lay on a sheet of greaseproof paper and repeat with the remaining cookies. Sprinkle the cookies with edible gold dust before the chocolate sets. Store in an airtight container and use within 2 weeks of making.

Mexican Fiesta Nueva

MENU FOR 6-8 GUESTS

APERITIF   Pomegranate Margarita

TO BE PASSED   Corn Fritters

With Roasted Tomato Sauce

Miniature Chilli Rellenos

With Chipotle Sauce

BUFFET   Build Your Own Tostada

'Fan Shell' Corn Tostada Shells

Grilled Steak, Chicken Breast and Cooked King Prawns

Grated Red Leicester and Cheddar Cheeses

Shredded Iceberg Lettuce, Spring Onions, Tomatoes and Sliced Avocado

Chipotle Peppers, Olives, Pico de Gallo and Papaya and Pineapple Salsas

Soured Cream and Guacamole

Mexican Red Rice

Chicken Enchiladas

With Cheese Sauce

Fire and Ice Salad

DESSERT   Kahlúa Chocolate Crêpes

With Hot Fudge Sauce

above Small clay pots of mini sunflowers hang from the limbs of an old California melaleuca tree behind an updated version of a Mexican buffet.

'Mark's Garden is one of the most elegant and exquisite florists I have ever used. Consistently over the top, always more than you could expect. The designers are so wonderfully talented with their use of colour and style that they actually seem to breathe life into their arrangements. Without exception, always stunning, and perfect for that special occasion. In short, Mark's Garden delivers... in more ways than one!'

Larry King

Southwest Chic

A contemporary California style is the approach we chose to present this very traditional Mexican menu. With a classic California-style Spanish patio as the setting, we have set out casual tables under parasols and taken our colour cues from the natural earth tones of the American southwest. Beige and terracotta tones are mixed with the muted green hues of local succulent plants and mosses. Hopsack linens with simple pottery dishes complemented by crisp linen napkins lend an unexpected fresh, modern look.

A mixture of succulent plants in dusky shades of green and red are gathered in a shallow clay bowl forming a miniature cactus garden as the centrepiece for this casual table. Twigs, branches and wood bark are combined as 'floral' elements to add some architectural structure to the piece. Small hand-blown shot glasses holding tiny cacti are added near each plate to unite the place settings with the centrepiece and offer a lovely take-home favour for each guest. Instead of a traditional piñata, small distressed clay pots sprouting mini-sunflowers and yellow daisies are strung from the ribs of the parasols to dangle fancifully overhead.

Pomegranate Margarita

MAKES 1 DRINK

60 ml tequila
30 ml pomegranate juice
20 ml freshly squeezed lemon or lime juice
pomegranate seeds, to garnish (optional)

Pour all of the ingredients into a glass tumbler filled with ice. Garnish with pomegranate seeds and serve immediately.

Miniature Chilli Rellenos with Chipotle Sauce

MAKES 18-24

250 g Cheddar cheese, cut into 2-cm cubes
8 tinned green chillies, cut into strips
4 eggs, separated
¼ teaspoon salt
2 tablespoons plain flour
vegetable oil, for deep frying
cocktail sticks, to serve

Heat the oil in a wok until very hot. Wrap the cheese cubes with a green chilli strip and secure with a cocktail stick. Beat the egg whites until very stiff. Beat the egg yolks well with 1 teaspoon water and salt and fold them into the whites. Fold in the flour. Dip each chilli cheese cube into the batter, making sure each one is well covered. Gently slide into the hot oil and fry until golden brown, turning to cook both sides. Do not crowd the wok. Remove with a slotted spoon and drain on kitchen paper. Serve hot with Chipotle Sauce.

CHIPOTLE SAUCE

MAKES 350 ml

200 ml good-quality mayonnaise
125 ml soured cream
2 tablespoons chipotle chillies in adobo sauce, finely chopped
sea salt and freshly ground black pepper

Put the ingredients in a medium bowl and stir to combine. Season to taste with salt and pepper. Will keep for 2-3 days if refrigerated in an airtight container

Corn Fritters with Roasted Tomato Sauce

MAKES 20-30 APPETIZERS

1 kg whole corn kernels (either cut fresh from the cob or frozen, do not use tinned)
1 egg, lightly beaten
4 spring onions, white part only, finely chopped
¼ teaspoon crushed garlic
2 tablespoons finely chopped coriander
350 g onion, finely chopped
150 g plain flour
125 g cornmeal
½ teaspoon salt
½ teaspoon baking powder
½ teaspoon ground coriander
corn oil, for frying

Heat the oil in a wok until very hot. Mix all of the ingredients together. Using two spoons or your fingers, drop small dollops into the oil and fry until golden brown. Remove with a slotted spoon and drain on kitchen paper. Serve warm with Roasted Tomato Sauce.

ROASTED TOMATO SAUCE

MAKES 750 ml

½ onion, coarsely chopped
3-4 garlic cloves
6-8 ripe red tomatoes, sliced in half
1 teaspoon smoked Spanish paprika (pimentón)
olive oil, to drizzle
chicken stock, to thin when blending
a handful of basil or parsley, chopped (optional)
freshly squeezed lemon juice (optional)
sea salt and freshly ground black pepper
a non-stick baking sheet

Preheat the oven to 190°C (375°F) Gas 5. Toss the onion, garlic, tomatoes, paprika and olive oil in bowl. Spread on the baking sheet and bake in the preheated oven until slightly caramelized and soft.

Purée the tomato mixture in a blender and add chicken stock slowly until the sauce is the desired consistency. Season to taste with salt and pepper. Stir in the herbs and a dash of lemon juice, if using.

Mexican Red Rice

SERVES 8-10

450 g long grain rice
125 ml vegetable oil
200 ml tomato passata
1 litre boiling water
1 teaspoon salt
½ teaspoon freshly ground black pepper

Several hours before serving, put the rice in hot water and leave to stand for 2-3 hours. Drain the water and allow the rice to dry on kitchen paper for about 1 hour.

Put the oil in a large pot, add the rice and fry until it is browned. Drain any excess oil. Add the tomato passata and simmer for 5 minutes over low heat, stirring constantly. Stir in the boiling water and season with salt and pepper. Cover and leave to cook over low heat for about 30 minutes, stirring occasionally, or until the rice is tender and all the water has been absorbed.

Chicken Enchiladas with Cheese Sauce

SERVES 8-10

For the filling:
3 large yellow onions, chopped
3 tablespoons oil or butter
6 poached chicken breasts, pulled into strips
375 g tinned green chillies, chopped
350 g Cheddar cheese, coarsely grated
    (reserve 120 g for topping enchiladas)
10-12 corn tortillas, warmed to soften
3 tablespoons oil

For the cheese sauce:
190 g butter
125 g flour
1½ teaspoons salt
1½ teaspoons white pepper
500 ml milk
375 ml chicken stock
375 ml soured cream
250 g Cheddar cheese, coarsely grated

To serve:
375 ml bottled green chilli salsa

3 medium tomatoes, chopped
1 avocado, sliced
a few sprigs of coriander
lime wedges, to serve
a large, rectangular baking dish, oiled

To make the cheese sauce, melt the butter in a saucepan, add the flour and stir until a light brown. Add the salt, pepper, milk and chicken stock. Cook until thickened. Add the soured cream and cheese. Season to taste.

Preheat the oven to 190°C (375°F) Gas 5. Sauté the onion in oil until lightly browned. Add the pulled chicken, green chillies and 230 g of Cheddar. Lay the tortillas flat and fill each one with about 125 g of the filling. Roll the tortillas and arrange in lines in the prepared dish. Pour cheese sauce over the top. Bake in the preheated oven for about 20 minutes or until lightly browned. Remove from the oven, sprinkle with the remaining Cheddar and return to the oven for 5 more minutes, or until the cheese has melted. Garnish with green chilli salsa, tomatoes, avocado, coriander and lime wedges.

Fire and Ice Salad

SERVES 8-10

200 g dark brown sugar
750 ml water
1 tablespoon dried chilli flakes
60 ml freshly squeezed lemon juice
2 mangos, peeled, stoned and cut into chunks
2 papayas, peeled, deseeded and cut into chunks
1 pineapple, peeled, cored and cut into chunks
6 small cucumbers, sliced
1 cantaloupe, peeled, deseeded and cut into chunks
1 honeydew, peeled, deseeded and cut into chunks
60 g basil, chopped
60 g mint, chopped
6 handfuls of watercress, washed

Put the sugar and water in a saucepan and simmer until the sugar has dissolved. Remove from the heat and add the chilli flakes and lemon juice.

Combine all the other ingredients, except the watercress, in a large salad bowl. Pour the sugar mixture over the fruit and toss to coat. Lay a bed of watercress on a platter and top with the fruit. Serve immediately.

Kahlúa Chocolate Crêpes

SERVES 8-10

250 g bitter dark chocolate, cut into chunks
350 ml whipping cream
125 ml Kahlúa, or to taste
whipped cream, to serve
dark chocolate shavings, to garnish
Hot Fudge Sauce (see page 74), to serve (optional)

For the crêpe batter:
125 g plain flour
1 tablespoon sugar
¼ teaspoon salt
3 eggs, lightly beaten
250 ml milk
100 ml water
40 g unsalted butter, melted
unsalted butter, for frying
a piping bag

First make the mousse. In a double boiler, slowly melt the dark chocolate. Be careful not to scorch with too high a heat. Once melted, remove from the heat and allow to cool, stirring occasionally. In a separate large, high-sided bowl, whip the whipping cream and Kahlúa until medium peaks form. Pour in ⅓ of the chocolate at a time and continue to whip to stiff peaks, being careful not to overbeat. Chill until needed.

To make the batter, sift the flour, sugar and salt into a large bowl. In a separate bowl, whisk the eggs, then add the milk, water and butter. Mix well. Add to the dry ingredients and combine until smooth. Cover with clingfilm and leave the batter to rest at room temperature for one hour. Heat a crêpe or omelette pan. Melt a little butter and swirl it round the pan to coat. Pour a little batter into the pan and swirl it around to make a thin film by quickly rotating and tilting the pan. When the underside is golden brown, flip with a spatula. Cook the other side for only a few seconds, it does not need to be brown. Stack the crêpes on a plate and cover with foil to keep warm.

To assemble, fill the piping bag with the chocolate mousse. Lay the crêpes on a flat surface and pipe a thick line of mousse down the centre. Fold the crêpes. Serve with whipped cream and Hot Fudge Sauce. Garnish with chocolate shavings.

A Rustic Italian Dinner

MENU FOR 6-8 GUESTS

APERITIF	Blood Orange Prosecco
TO BE PASSED	Fried Sage Leaves
	With Italian Sausage and Parmesan Cheese Filling

BUFFET   Antipasti Platter

A Selection of Italian Cheeses to include Gorgonzola and Soft Goats' Cheese

A Variety of Salami and Meats to include Soppressata, Bresaola and Prosciutto

Marinated Artichoke Hearts, Marinated Olives, Cerignola Olives, Roasted Red
and Golden Beetroots, Grilled Red and Yellow Peppers and Fresh Figs

Served with a Basket of Breadsticks and Seeded Cracker Breads

Sautéed Prawns with Orange 'Dust'

Served on a Bed of Lemon, Orange and Lime Wheels

Turkey Breast with Pancetta

And White Wine Sauce

DESSERT   Grand Marnier Chocolate Stuffed Figs

Sgroppino

above left A compote of kumquats and fresh herb topiaries accent the table décor.

above right A hollowed artichoke makes a unique and attractive vase for orange ranunculus.

'Mark's Garden exhibits an artistry that I have rarely seen by another florist. They are capable of producing extravagant and magnificent floral designs that transform a room and evoke a spirit of their own. They can also create precious one-of-a-kind objets d'art incorporating natural and unexpected materials that are a joy to behold. They have provided many gorgeous creations for my family over the years and we are always thrilled with their work. In the world of design there is nothing else like them.'

Oscar de la Renta

Benvenuto!

The mention of an Italian dinner conjures images of a warm, convivial group gathered for a good time and that was exactly the sense we had going into this. We selected a beautiful rustic setting and bright earthy tones of deep reds, terracotta, rust and orange to capture the mood and spirit of this party. We know there is to be a lot of great food so we set a large table with a relaxed and casual feel, inviting our guests to sit and talk and eat as long as they want.

Red and terracotta roses, yellow-tipped orange tulips and orange ranunculus in vintage clay pots share the table with herb topiaries, moss and bowls of kumquats to provide an authentic feel without resorting to the expected standby for Italian décor like sunflowers or daisies. In our usual pursuit of something new, we also decided to use linen panels interwoven across the table rather than a standard tablecloth. These panels are handy to have because they can be used in so many different ways. The buffet table is a cascade of roses flowing from a wire pillar on to the table and surrounding the food. For a whimsical touch, we covered a bench with moss and ferns of varying shades of green, more as a unique décor touch than for seating.

Blood Orange Prosecco
MAKES 8 DRINKS
350 ml blood orange juice, strained and chilled
1 x 750-ml bottle of Prosecco or sparkling wine, well chilled
8 thin slices of blood orange, to garnish (optional)
8 Champagne flutes or similar, well chilled

Pour 3 tablespoons blood orange juice into a chilled Champagne flute. Slowly pour in the chilled Prosecco.

Garnish each glass with a slice of blood orange, if using. Serve immediately.

Fried Sage Leaves with Italian Sausage and Parmesan Cheese Filling

MAKES 25 APPETIZERS

48 sage leaves
125 g Parmesan cheese, finely grated
250 g Italian sausagemeat
2 eggs, beaten
250 g Japanese Panko or other dry breadcrumbs
light vegetable oil, for deep frying

Wash the sage leaves and pat dry. Heat the oil in a wok or large pot until very hot. Top a sage leaf with 1 teaspoon Parmesan cheese and 1–2 teaspoons sausagemeat. Press another sage leaf on top of the cheese and sausage. Dip each sage leaf in the egg and roll in breadcrumbs. Deep fry until golden brown and the sausage is cooked. Serve with Roasted Tomato Sauce (see page 105) but omit the pimentón from the recipe.

Sautéed Prawns with Orange 'Dust'

SERVES 8–10

3 oranges, plus 2 for garnish
3 lemons, plus 2 for garnish
3 limes, plus 2 for garnish
2 tablespoons paprika
2 tablespoons onion powder
1 tablespoon sea salt
1 tablespoon finely chopped shallots
3 tablespoons vegetable oil
3 tablespoons butter
24–32 large raw prawns, shells and veins removed, tails on
salt and freshly ground black pepper

Grate the zest from the oranges, lemons and limes. Save the flesh and squeeze the juice into a separate container. Set aside. Mix the grated zest with the paprika, onion powder and salt. Spread the zest mixture onto a baking sheet, and leave to dry at room temperature for 3–4 hours or overnight. Sauté the shallots in oil and butter over medium heat until soft. Add the prawns, half of the zest mixture and reserved citrus juice. Continue to sauté until the prawns are opaque. Season to taste with salt and pepper. Slice the remaining citrus fruit to garnish and arrange on the bottom of a large platter. Top with the cooked prawns and sprinkle with additional zest mixture to taste.

Antipasti Platter

SERVES 8

250–300 g Gorgonzola
250–300 g soft goats' cheese
12–16 slices bresaola
12–16 slices soppressata salami
12–16 slices prosciutto
2 red peppers, roasted, skin removed, deseeded and sliced
2 yellow peppers, roasted, skin removed, deseeded and sliced
350 g marinated artichoke hearts
350 g marinated olives and/or cerignola olives
1 large golden beetroot, roasted, peeled and diced
1 large red beetroot, roasted, peeled and diced
2–3 fresh figs, quartered
a handful of basil leaves
1 bunch flat leaf parsley, chopped
olive oil, to drizzle
Italian breadsticks and seeded cracker bread, to serve

Arrange all the ingredients on a large platter and garnish with basil leaves and parsley. Drizzle with olive oil. Serve with a basket of Italian breadsticks (grissini) and seeded cracker bread.

Turkey Breast with Pancetta and White Wine Sauce

SERVES 8–10

1 (1.8–2.25 kg) boneless turkey breast
250 g pancetta or streaky bacon
30 g parsley, chopped
60 g basil, chopped
1 tablespoon sea salt
1 tablespoon cracked black pepper
8–10 lengths of kitchen string

Preheat the oven to 170°C (325°F) Gas 3. Pound the turkey breast to flatten slightly. Layer the pancetta, parsley, basil, salt and pepper on top. Roll the turkey breast lengthways and tie with kitchen string.

Place in a roasting tin and in the preheated oven to cook for about 3 hours or until a thermometer inserted into the meat reads 71°C. Remove from the oven and leave to rest for 5 minutes. Slice and serve with White Wine Sauce.

WHITE WINE SAUCE

MAKES APPROXIMATELY 450 ml

100 g unsalted butter
35 g plain flour
450 ml white wine
450 ml chicken stock
2 tablespoons white balsamic vinegar
2 tablespoons freshly squeezed lemon juice
4 shallots, finely chopped
1 teaspoon each of finely chopped thyme,
   rosemary and sage
sea salt and freshly ground black pepper

In a large frying pan over medium heat, melt the butter and whisk in the flour to make a light brown roux.

In a separate heavy, large sauté pan, bring the white wine, chicken stock, white balsamic vinegar, lemon juice and shallots to the boil. Reduce the heat, add the chopped herbs and leave to simmer until reduced by half. Slowly whisk in the roux to create the desired consistency. Season to taste with salt and pepper and serve while still hot.

Grand Marnier Chocolate Stuffed Figs

MAKES 24–36 FIGS

250 ml double cream
250 g dark bitter chocolate, finely chopped
2 tablespoons Grand Marnier
24–36 fresh figs
700 g dark chocolate (sweetened)
a piping bag fitted with a small round nozzle

Heat the cream in a saucepan over medium/high heat until it just begins to boil. Remove from the heat and add the 250 g chocolate and Grand Marnier. Stir until smooth and pour the mixture into a bowl. Cover with clingfilm (so that it touches the top of the chocolate) and leave to set for 6–8 hours at room temperature.

Use a skewer to enlarge the hole in the base of each fig. When the ganache is set, gently stir it with a plastic spatula to loosen. Transfer to the piping bag. Pipe each fig full of the mixture. Chill for at least an hour.

In a double boiler, gently melt the remaining chocolate and let cool, stirring occasionally. Dip the bottom half of the figs in the melted chocolate and place on a parchment-lined baking sheet. Let set at room temperature. Serve within a few hours of making.

Sgroppino

SERVES 8–10

750 ml whipping cream
125 ml freshly squeezed lemon juice
350 g sugar
3 tablespoons finely grated lemon zest
1 bottle Prosecco or other sparkling white wine
   (750 ml), well chilled
candied lemon peel and/or mint sprigs, to garnish

In a large bowl, mix the cream, lemon juice, sugar and lemon zest until blended. Pour into a shallow dish, cover and freeze overnight or for several days.

Before serving, take the lemon ice cream out of the freezer to soften. Transfer to a large bowl and roughly mash or break up with a whisk. Gradually whisk in the Prosecco to your preferred thickness. Spoon into a Martini glass, garnish as desired and serve immediately.

A Green Tea

MENU FOR 8-10

TO DRINK	Frozen Kiwi Daiquiri
	A Selection of Fine Teas
TO BE PASSED	Crab Salad on Brioche Toast
	With Wasabi Caviar
	Chicory with Goats' Cheese
SAVOURY TABLE	Open Face Tea Sandwiches
	Cucumber Curls, Coriander Chutney and Herby Cream Cheese
	Crab with Red Pepper Chutney
	Prawn Cocktail and Fresh Dill
	Closed Face Tea Sandwiches
	Rare Roast Beef with Watercress and Horseradish Sauce
	Chicken Salad with Tarragon
	Devilled Egg with Fresh Dill
	Tomato and Cucumber with Herby Cream Cheese
	Ham and Baby Salad Leaves with Honey Mustard
SWEET TABLE	Warm Anne Boleyn Tarts
	Meringue Kisses with Kiwi Fruit Fool
	Coconut Cake
	With Lemon Curd and Whipped Vanilla Cream

left Cascades of orchids and tropical greenery recreate equatorial splendour as the setting for our green party.

Mother Nature Rules

Here is a tea party to raise awareness and pay tribute to the natural environment. With this all-green theme we demonstrate the beauty and splendour of nature, embracing within our décor many plants and wildlife ranging from the tropical rainforests, to the jungles and the plains of Africa. Combining species of green flora from all around the world we remind ourselves of the precious nature of our own being as well as that of all the things on the planet.

A majestic hand-made tree of willow branches sweeps upwards from the centre of the table, merging a dense growth of vines, ferns and moss with exotic orchids, tropical anthurium and venus flytraps. Our table is covered with a natural green silk linen over a skirt of real magnolia leaves and set with Hermès' delicate 'Africa' pattern china featuring wild animals. At every place setting a tiny seedling tree in a tied hessian bag is presented to each guest to take home for planting. In the background we have filled large shells mounted on the walls with gracefully draping amaranthus and dendrobium orchids. The buffet display is a mixture of poppy pods, green calla lilies, green zinnia, green anthurium and mixed exotic ferns.

Frozen Kiwi Daiquiri
MAKES 20 DRINKS

350 g frozen lemonade concentrate, thawed
175 g frozen limeade concentrate, thawed
1 bottle light rum (750 ml)
500–750 ml ready-made kiwi purée
lime or kiwi slices, to garnish

Combine all the ingredients, except the kiwi purée, with 750 ml water in a large container and freeze for 24 hours. When ready to serve, remove from the freezer and break up with a spoon. Add kiwi purée to taste and stir. Serve in your choice of well-chilled glass, garnished as desired.

Crab Salad on Brioche Toast
MAKES 18-20

1 teaspoon grated lemon zest
2 tablespoons freshly squeezed lemon juice
3 tablespoons extra virgin olive oil
450 g lump crabmeat, picked over for cartilage
50 g spring onions, thinly sliced
1–2 tablespoons good-quality mayonnaise (optional)
125 g wasabi caviar
salt and freshly ground black pepper

In a bowl, combine the lemon zest, lemon juice and olive oil. Season with salt and pepper. Add the crab and spring onions and mix to combine. Add a small amount of mayonnaise to bind the mixture, if desired. Cover and refrigerate.

To serve, pile a couple of teaspoons of crab salad on top of each Brioche Toast. Finish with wasabi caviar.

BRIOCHE TOASTS
MAKES 50-60 TOASTS

1 Brioche loaf, crusts removed, cut into
  1-cm slices and each slice quartered
125 g butter, melted

Preheat the oven to 200°C (400°F) Gas 6. Brush both sides of the bread with butter. Place on a baking sheet and cook for 5–10 minutes until brown and crisp. Keep the leftovers in an airtight container for up to 1 week.

Tea Sandwiches

Tasty little tea sandwiches are a doddle to make. Use your favourite bakery's bread and ask if they will slice the bread vertically. A variety of breads and fillings is appealing and adds interest to a tea table.

Flavour softened butter with herbs, curry paste, chilli sauce, horseradish or other savoury choices. Prepare several fillings such as chicken and chutney, egg salad, devilled ham, crab or prawn salad and thinly sliced roast beef, ham, turkey, lamb, pork, cheeses, tomatoes and cucumbers.

Remove the crusts from the bread. Spread all the slices with softened butter and spread your sandwich filling on half the slices. Top with the remaining bread slices. Cut the sandwiches into squares, rectangles or triangles, or even make cut-out novelty shapes with cookie cutters.

If you like, butter some of the sandwich edges with softened butter and dip in toasted nuts or chopped herbs. Sandwiches can be made several hours ahead of time. To keep them moist, cover with kitchen paper, spray lightly with water and cover with clingfilm.

Chicory with Goats' Cheese

MAKES 36

2 x 150-g logs soft goats' cheese,
   at room temperature
250 g cream cheese, at room temperature
½ teaspoon Tabasco or other hot sauce
350 g roasted or sun-dried tomatoes
4–5 heads chicory, leaves separated,
   rinsed and chilled
1 bunch chives, cut into 2.5-cm lengths

Combine the goats' cheese, cream cheese
and Tabasco. Chop the tomatoes. Add any
tomato marinade to the cheese and mix.
Put 1 tablespoon cheese mixture on each
leaf and garnish with chopped tomatoes
and chives. Refrigerate until ready to serve.

Warm Anne Boleyn Tarts

MAKES 24 TARTS

2 sheets frozen puff pastry, thawed and rolled
60 g cottage cheese
40 g butter, softened
2 eggs, beaten
3 tablespoons brandy
125 g granulated sugar
60 g mashed potato (instant is suitable)
40 g almonds, toasted and ground
grated zest of 2 unwaxed lemons
½ teaspoon nutmeg
3 tablespoons freshly squeezed lemon juice
icing sugar or lemon glaze, for topping
2 x 12-hole cupcake tins, greased
a small cookie cutter

Preheat the oven to 180°C (350°F) Gas 4.
Cut out 24 small rounds of pastry and press
them down into the holes in the prepared
cupcake tins. In a mixer, beat the cottage
cheese and butter together. Add the eggs,
brandy and sugar and mix well. In a separate
bowl, beat together the potato, almonds,
lemon zest, nutmeg and lemon juice.
Gradually blend in the cheese mixture. Beat
thoroughly. Spoon the filling into the pastry
shells and bake for 25–30 minutes or until
set. Sift icing sugar over the tarts, or mix
together sugar and lemon juice to make a
glaze to drizzle over the top. Serve warm.

Meringue Kisses with Kiwi Fruit Fool

MAKES 30–35

8 large egg whites
¾ teaspoon salt
450 g granulated sugar
a pastry bag fitted with a plain nozzle
2 baking trays lined with greaseproof paper

KIWI FRUIT FOOL

250 ml double cream
120 g icing sugar
125 ml soured cream or crème fraîche
4 kiwi fruit, mashed

Preheat the oven to its lowest setting.

Beat the egg whites and salt in a mixer on
high speed until they just hold stiff peaks.
Gradually add the sugar. Continue to beat
on high until the whites hold stiff, glossy
peaks. Spoon into the pastry bag and pipe
2.5-cm kisses onto the prepared baking
sheets. Bake until dry, about 2 hours.

To make the fool, beat the double cream in
a mixer until soft peaks form. Gradually add
the sugar and beat until stiff peaks hold.
Gently fold in the soured cream and mashed
kiwi fruit. Serve the Meringue Kisses with
the Kiwi Fruit Fool as a dip.

Coconut Cake

MAKES A 23-CM ROUND CAKE

175 g unsalted butter, room temperature
325 g sugar
240 g plain flour
2 teaspoons baking powder
¼ teaspoon salt
3 large eggs plus 1 yolk
180 ml milk
3 teaspoons vanilla extract
lemon curd (see right) and whipped
   vanilla cream (see right)
desiccated coconut, to fill and decorate
2 x 23-cm round cake tins, greased and lined
with greaseproof paper

Preheat the oven to 180°C (350°F) Gas 4.
In a large bowl, beat the butter and sugar
until light and fluffy. In a separate bowl, sift
and mix the flour, baking powder and salt. In
a third bowl, combine all the eggs, milk and
vanilla extract. Add a third of the flour mixture
to the butter mixture, then add half the milk
mixture. Repeat, ending with the last third of
flour mixture, scraping down the bowl often.

Pour into the prepared tins and bake for
25–30 minutes, or until the centre springs
back when lightly pressed. Leave to cool in
the tins for 5 minutes, then turn out on to
a wire rack and leave to cool completely.

Trim the sides and top of each cake to make
even. Top one cake with lemon curd, add
whipped cream and coconut, and put the
second cake on top. Frost with whipped
cream and decorate all over with coconut.

LEMON CURD

MAKES ABOUT 870 ML

8 egg yolks
325 g sugar
zest and freshly squeezed juice of 6 unwaxed
lemons, plus extra juice to make 125 ml, if needed
175 g butter, cold and cut into cubes

Bring a few centimetres of water to a simmer
in a pan. In a metal bowl, whisk together the
egg yolks, sugar, lemon juice and zest until
smooth. Put over the simmering water and
continue to whisk until thick and light yellow,
about 10 minutes. Remove from heat and
whisk in the butter, 2 cubes at a time.
When the butter is completely incorporated,
transfer to a container, and cover the
surface of the curd with a layer of clingfilm.
Refrigerate overnight and up to 2 weeks.

WHIPPED VANILLA CREAM

750 ml whipping cream
2 tablespoons vanilla extract
150 g icing sugar

In a mixing bowl, whip the cream and vanilla
to soft peaks. Gradually add the sugar and
whip to stiff peaks. Refrigerate until needed.

Californian Wine Tasting

MENU FOR 6–8 GUESTS

TO DRINK	A Tasting of Wine from the Henry Wine Group
TO BE SET OUT	Blue Cheese Terrine

Blue Cheese Terrine
With Roasted Grapes and Rosemary Cashew Nuts

Smoked Salmon and Provolone Loaf
With Dill and Capers

Crab Mousse

Panini in Paper
Pesto Chicken; Brie and Prosciutto; Smoked Salmon and Cream Cheese

Carol Henry's Prawns
With Ginger and Herb Butter

'The Kitchen's' Cheese Toast

Fine Wines

right We employ robust jewel tone colours and shades of green to tie into the beautiful natural surroundings and, of course, bunches of grapes that we incorporate into the décor.

When we think of wine today we not only imagine French and Italian countrysides but our own Napa Valley where some of the finest wines in the world are now grown. When we found this location in our own 'backyard' we immediately recognized what a perfect setting it would be for our wine tasting party. We wanted it to be casual but elegant to reflect the sophisticated wines and menu we planned, so we have set up a table under a soaring oak tree. Large buffet arrangements burst with deep red and hot orange roses mixed with red Gloriosa lilies,

purple scabiosa and alium, red dahlias, orange tulips and green viburnum. The arrangements and the table are draped with cascades of red and green grapes and the tapestry-covered table is entwined with live grape vines, ivy and moss. The floral highlights, however, are the deep red rose 'glamellias' mounted on Tag Anderson-designed metal flutes rising above the table. Glamellias are wonderfully oversized blooms hand-made from individually applied rose petals attached to a foam base. They are a Mark's Garden signature design.

'The Kitchen's' Cheese Toast

MAKES ABOUT 36 SLICES

450 ml good-quality mayonnaise
250 g Parmesan cheese, grated
3 tablespoons finely chopped shallots
6 day-old bread rolls, thinly sliced

Preheat the oven to 180°C (350°F) Gas 4.
Combine the mayonnaise, cheese and
shallots. Spread approximately 1 tablespoon
of the mixture on each slice of bread. Bake
in the oven for 4–5 minutes, or until golden
brown. These toasts will keep fresh in an
airtight container for at least 1 week.

Smoked Salmon and Provolone Loaf

MAKES 1 LOAF, SERVES 12

450 g cream cheese
125 ml crème fraîche
2 tablespoons freshly squeezed lemon juice
12–16 slices provolone cheese
450–700 g smoked salmon, sliced
1 bunch dill, chopped
100 g capers, rinsed
cucumber curls, to garnish (optional)
flatbreads and crackers, to serve
a medium loaf tin lined with clingfilm
to extend over the edges

In a mixer, beat together the cream cheese,
crème fraîche and lemon juice until well
combined. Set aside.

Line the prepared loaf tin with the slices of
provolone cheese. Spread one-third of the
cream cheese mixture over the provolone
and sprinkle with dill and capers. Line with
a few slices of smoked salmon. Repeat
layers ending in a layer of provolone. Fold
clingfilm over the pan to cover and chill in
the refrigerator for several hours.

To serve, pull back the clingfilm and turn
upside down on a serving platter. Take the
loaf tin off and pull back the rest of the
clingfilm. Top with the remaining salmon.
Garnish with additional dill, capers and
cucumber curls if desired. Serve with
flatbreads and crackers.

Crab Mousse

SERVES 10

125 ml dry white wine
2 packs unflavoured powdered gelatine
1 tablespoon very finely chopped shallots
1 tablespoon freshly squeezed lemon juice
2 tablespoons chilli sauce
250 ml good-quality mayonnaise
125 g crabmeat, plus extra to garnish
180 ml whipping cream
sea salt and freshly ground black pepper
finely sliced spring onions, to garnish
crackers and/or brioche toasts, to serve
a cake or loaf tin lined with clingfilm
to extend over the edges, lightly oiled

Pour the wine into a saucepan and add the
gelatine. Heat until the gelatine has melted.
Set aside and leave to cool.

In a large mixing bowl, combine the shallots,
lemon juice, chilli sauce and mayonnaise
until well blended. Add the slightly cooled
gelatine mixture, crab and whipping cream,
and gently fold the ingredients together.
Season to taste with salt and pepper.
Pour into the prepared cake tin, cover with
clingfilm and refrigerate. After the mousse
has set, carefully unmould onto a serving
platter and garnish with crab and sliced
spring onions. Serve with crackers or
brioche toasts.

Carol Henry's Prawns with Ginger and Herb Butter

SERVES 10

90 g butter, at room temperature
15 g coriander, chopped
3 cloves garlic, crushed
2 tablespoons chopped chives
2 teaspoons grated fresh ginger
2 teaspoons sesame oil
24 uncooked large prawns, peeled and deveined
sea salt and freshly ground black pepper
lime wedges, to serve

Mix the first 6 ingredients in small bowl until
well blended and season to taste with salt
and pepper. Melt the butter mixture in a
sauté pan. Add the prawns and sauté until
opaque in the centre, about 3 minutes.
Serve warm with fresh lime wedges.

Panini in Paper
EACH RECIPE MAKES 8–10 PANINI
You will need a panini press,
greaseproof paper and string.

Pesto Chicken:
3 cloves garlic
75 g pine nuts
175 g Parmesan cheese, grated
175 g loosely packed basil
150 ml extra virgin olive oil, plus extra for brushing
sea salt and freshly ground black pepper
3 chicken breasts, cooked, cooled and shredded
125 g small rocket leaves
1 loaf ciabatta bread, sliced in half lengthways

To make the pesto, put the garlic in a food
processor and pulse until finely chopped.
Add 50 g pine nuts, 120 g cheese, the
basil, 1 teaspoon salt, ½ teaspoon pepper,
and process until finely chopped. With the
motor running, add the oil in a slow and
steady stream, blending until well combined.
Adjust seasoning if necessary. Combine the
shredded chicken, pesto and remaining
cheese and pine nuts in a bowl. Season to
taste and add the rocket.

Heat the panini press. Spread the chicken
mixture on the bread, close and brush both
sides with olive oil. Cook in the press for
3–4 minutes, until the crust is golden
and crispy. Cut into bite-sized squares or
rectangles. Wrap with paper and tie with
string. Serve warm.

Brie and Prosciutto:
60 ml good-quality mayonnaise
1 loaf ciabatta bread, sliced in half lengthways
250 g brie, cut into slices
½ small red onion, thinly sliced
120 g prosciutto, very thinly sliced
olive oil, for brushing

Heat the panini press. Spread mayonnaise
on both cut sides of the bread and arrange
the brie, onion and prosciutto on one side.
Close and brush with olive oil.

Cook in the panini press for 3–4 minutes,
until the crust is golden and crispy. Cut into
bite-sized squares or rectangles. Wrap with
paper and tie with string. Serve warm.

Smoked Salmon and Cream Cheese:
125 g Boursin cheese (or a cream cheese with
    garlic and herbs of your choice)
250 g smoked salmon, thinly sliced
½ small red onion, thinly sliced
40 g capers, rinsed
1 loaf ciabatta bread, sliced in half lengthways
olive oil, for brushing

Heat the panini press. Spread the cheese
on both cut sides of the bread and arrange
the salmon and red onion on one side and
sprinkle with capers. Close and brush both
sides with olive oil.

Cook in the panini press for 3–4 minutes,
until the crust is golden and crispy. Cut into
bite-sized squares or rectangles. Wrap with
paper and tie with string. Serve warm.

Blue Cheese Terrine
SERVES 10
450 g firm blue cheese, crumbled
70 g soft fresh goats' cheese
70 g cream cheese, at room temperature
60 g butter, at room temperature
2 tablespoons brandy
Rosemary Cashew Nuts and/or Roasted Grapes
    (see below), to garnish
crackers and bread, to serve
a cake or loaf tin, lightly oiled, lined
with clingfilm to extend over the edges

Combine the blue cheese, goats' cheese,
cream cheese and butter in a processor
and blend until smooth. Stir in the brandy.
Spoon the mixture into the prepared cake
tin and refrigerate overnight.

Carefully unmould the cheese onto a serving
platter and top with Rosemary Cashew Nuts
and/or Roasted Grapes. Serve with crackers
and bread.

ROASTED GRAPES
SERVES 6–8
450 g red and/or green seedless grapes
2 tablespoons balsamic vinegar
1 tablespoon grapeseed oil

Preheat the oven to 190°C (375°F) Gas 5.
Spread the grape clusters out on a baking
tray. Drizzle with vinegar and oil. Roast in the
preheated oven for 12 minutes or until the
grape skins are slightly blistered. Serve the
grapes warm or at room temperature.

ROSEMARY CASHEW NUTS
SERVES 6–8
60 g rosemary, finely chopped
2 tablespoons olive oil
450 g roasted and salted cashew nuts

Preheat the oven to 230°C (450°F) Gas 8.
On a baking tray, toss the rosemary and oil
with the nuts. Roast in the preheated oven
for 10–12 minutes. Serve the nuts warm or
at room temperature.

Chocolate & Coffee Party

MENU FOR 8–10 GUESTS

APERITIF	White Russian
DESSERT COFFEE BAR	Create Your Own Flavourful Gourmet Coffee
DESSERT TABLE	Torta Cavour

With Kahlúa Crème

Chocolate Brownie Tarts

Ginger Crème Sandwich Biscuits

With Ginger Crème Filling

Miniature Pavlova

With Passion Fruit Crème

Chocolate Espresso Malts

Served in Chocolate Cups

Pure Indulgence

Chocolate and coffee – two of the most favoured and craved food items in the world. Chocolate releases endorphins in the brain and makes you feel happy. Caffeine in coffee gives you energy. What great elements for a party! Not only are they great food elements, they make for beautiful décor. So for this party we are making it look as good as it tastes by doing everything in tones of chocolate, coffee and cream.

Atop a brown suede-covered table, we let the chocolate do the talking as 'eye candy' and accent our luscious desserts with a few small vases of hypericum, also known as coffee bean, brown roses, brown rudbekia, brown orchids and chocolate cosmos (yes, they actually smell like chocolate!). We even use slabs of pure chocolate on the table for decoration. The dishware we have chosen has an appetizing chocolate-brown swirl pattern to complete the theme.

above An unexpected nosegay of thorny rudbekia matches the brown and gold tones of our chocolate-inspired theme.

Torta Cavour
MAKES 1 LARGE 3-LAYER MERINGUE
For the meringues:
12 large egg whites, at room temperature
½ teaspoon cream of tartar
a pinch of salt
1½ teaspoons vanilla extract
700 g sugar
90 g chestnut flour or cornflour

For the filling:
1 litre double cream
250 g granulated sugar
60 ml Kahlúa or Amaretto
175 g toasted flaked almonds
400 g dark chocolate, coarsely chopped
greaseproof paper with 3 x 25-cm
traced circles
3 baking trays
a pastry bag

Preheat the oven to its lowest setting.
Place the egg whites, cream of tartar, salt
and vanilla in a large mixing bowl and beat
until frothy and the mixture holds soft peaks.
Gradually beat in sugar about 100 g at a
time. Continue beating at high speed until
the whites are glossy and thick. Pour the
chestnut flour over the egg whites and fold
in with a plastic spatula just until combined.

Fill a pastry bag with the meringue. Place
the tip of the bag on the perimeter of one
of the paper circles and start piping the
meringue. Continue piping in decreasing
circles to the centre. Fill all circles alike.
Place in the preheated oven for about
2 hours, until the meringues are crisp and
dry. Leave to cool before filling. To make the
filling, put the cream in a large, chilled bowl
and whip it, gradually beating in the sugar
until soft peaks form. Add the liqueur a little
at a time and beat until medium peaks form.

To assemble, place a meringue round on
a serving tray. Spread with some cream and
sprinkle with about ⅓ of the almonds and
chocolate and press lightly into the cream.
Repeat with another layer of meringue. Top
with the final layer and finish with remaining
cream, almonds and chocolate. This dessert
may be prepared a day in advance and
allowed to mellow in the refrigerator.

Dessert Coffee Bar
Prepare decaffeinated and regular coffee
with dark espresso coffee beans. Select
a variety of liqueurs: Nocello, Kahlúa,
Bailey's Irish Cream, Amaretto, Godiva
Chocolate Liqueur and various brandies.
Choose accompaniments such as coffee-
flavoured sweets, dark and white sugar
swizzle sticks, flavoured sugar cubes, dark
and white chocolate chips, chocolate
cigarettes, cinnamon sticks, an array of
tuiles, whipped cream and silver shakers
filled with cocoa, cinnamon and icing sugar.
Create an attractive display and let your
guests make their own artisanal coffee.

White Russian
MAKES 1 DRINK
30 ml Kahlúa
30 ml vodka
1 shot freshly-made espresso
100 ml whipping cream, lightly whipped
chocolate shavings, to garnish

Pour the Kahlúa, vodka and espresso in a
serving glass of your choice and top with
whipped cream. Garnish with chocolate
shavings. Serve immediately.

Chocolate Brownie Tarts

SERVES 8-10

90 g unsalted butter
500 g dark chocolate, chopped
3 large eggs
250 g granulated sugar
2 tablespoons instant coffee or 2 shots espresso
1 teaspoon vanilla extract
60 g flour
¼ teaspoon baking powder
¼ teaspoon salt
125 g toasted pecans or hazelnuts, chopped
175 g white or dark chocolate chips
icing sugar, to dust
fresh raspberries, to garnish
8-10 individual tart tins, greased
and lightly floured

Preheat the oven to 180°C (350°F) Gas 4.
Melt the butter and chocolate in a double
boiler. Leave to cool. Beat the eggs, sugar,
coffee and vanilla extract together until the
mixture is light and fluffy. Mix in the butter
and chocolate mixture. Sift together the flour,
baking powder and salt. Fold the flour
mixture into the egg and chocolate mixture.
Add the nuts and chocolate chips. Spoon
into the prepared tart tins. Bake in the
preheated oven for 20-25 minutes. Serve
warm, dusted with icing sugar and garnished
with fresh raspberries. Alternatively, add a
scoop of vanilla ice cream and Hot Fudge
Sauce (see page 74).

Ginger Crème Sandwich Biscuits

MAKES 48 BISCUITS

175 g unsalted butter
250 g granulated sugar
50 ml molasses
1 large egg
250 g plain flour
2 teaspoons bicarbonate of soda
½ teaspoon salt
1 teaspoon icing sugar
½ teaspoon ground cloves
1 teaspoon cinnamon

For the ginger crème:
280 g icing sugar
50 g crystallized ginger, finely chopped
50 g butter, at room temperature
a little cream or milk, to blend

Over medium heat, melt the butter in a large
saucepan. Stir in the sugar and molasses.
Add the egg and whisk well. Sift together
the remaining ingredients and gradually stir
into the molasses mixture until combined.
Chill for several hours in the refrigerator.

Preheat the oven to 190°C (375°F) Gas 5.
Pinch and form the chilled dough into
2.5-cm balls. Place on a baking tray
and bake for 8-10 minutes.

To make the ginger crème, blend together
the sugar, ginger and butter. Add sufficient
cream or milk to the mixture to obtain
a spreadable consistency.

To assemble, spread a tablespoon of ginger
crème on a biscuit and top with another to
make a sandwich. The filled biscuits will stay
crisp for several hours.

Miniature Pavlova with Passion Fruit Crème

MAKES 16-20 SMALL MERINGUES

8 large egg whites
¾ teaspoon salt
a pinch of cream of tartar
500 g granulated sugar
375 ml double cream
75 g icing sugar
175 g ready-made passion fruit purée
raspberries, figs, redcurrants and physalis,
    to garnish
a few sprigs of mint, to garnish
a pastry bag
a baking tray lined with greaseproof paper

Preheat oven to its lowest setting. Beat the
egg whites, salt and cream of tartar until soft
peaks form. Gradually add the sugar until
the mixture is glossy and holds stiff peaks.
Spoon the meringue into a pastry bag and
pipe 8-cm circles on the prepared baking
sheet. Make a small indentation in each one
with a spoon. Bake in the preheated oven
for about 2 hours, until dry.

Whip the cream to medium peaks and
gradually add the icing sugar. Fold in the
passion fruit purée. Fill the meringue shells
with a few tablespoons of the cream and
passion fruit mixture. Top with fruit and
garnish with sprigs of mint.

Chocolate Espresso Malts

MAKES 8-10

500 ml chocolate ice cream
2 tablespoons powdered malt
60 ml milk
2 shots espresso, chilled
1 shot Kahlúa (optional)
8-10 espresso cups or edible chocolate cups*
whipped cream, chocolate shavings and cinnamon
    sticks, to garnish

Put the ice cream, malt, milk, espresso and
Kahlúa in a blender and blend to combine.
Pour into cups and garnish with whipped
cream, chocolate shavings and a cinnamon
stick as a stirrer.

*Note: Edible chocolate espresso cups may
be found at specialist chocolate shops and
online suppliers.

April Showers for Baby

MENU FOR 8–10

TO DRINK	Blue 'Hpnotiq' Martini
	Samantha Ruby's Sparkling Berry Lemonade
	A Selection of Fine Teas
TO BE PASSED	Creamy Goats' Cheese
	With Roasted Tomatoes
	Served on a Crispy Spoon-shaped Cracker
STARTER	Mushroom Consommé
	With Enoki Mushrooms
MAIN COURSE	Chicken and Pesto Salad with Rocket
DESSERT	Chocolate Cupcakes with Vanilla Buttercream
	Vanilla Cupcakes with Vanilla Buttercream
	Checkerboard Cookies
	For a Baby Boy or Girl

right A topiary stork welcomes guests to the buffet table with moss and flowers nestled among the platters of food.

Baby Blues

Baby showers were primarily an American tradition until recent years but their popularity has spread around the world. We call this our 'April Showers' party and use colourful inverted umbrellas, trimmed with flowers and raining streams of hyacinth blossoms. Of course pink and blue are the traditional colours but we push it a bit, departing from the customary pastels and moving into deeper shades of these hues. We even have pink and blue food and drinks! You could use this same umbrella theme for any spring party and your guests would be equally delighted. Upside-down umbrellas mounted to poles stand in the centre of each table and a chain of separated hyacinth blossoms 'drip' on to the table. The umbrellas have been covered in custom fabrics coordinated to the floral colours and at the base of each, is a bountiful garden of blooms. Nearly every available spring flower has been included, from roses and peonies to hydrangea and sweet peas. Inside each cone-shaped napkin roll is tucked a nosegay of sweet peas and at each place setting a charming individual teapot holds each guest's choice of tea and becomes their parting gift. An ivy topiary stork is perched on a nearby table as a symbol of the event.

Blue 'Hpnotiq' Martini
MAKES 1 DRINK
175 ml Hpnotiq
a splash of 7-up (or other clear lemonade)
freshly squeezed lemon juice, to taste

Add all the ingredients to a cocktail
shaker filled with ice, shake and strain
into a cocktail glass rimmed with blue
crystallized sugar.

Samantha Ruby's Sparkling Berry Lemonade
MAKES 1 COCKTAIL
6-8 fresh raspberries
2-3 fresh strawberries
granulated sugar, to taste
45 ml freshly squeezed lemon juice
50 ml sugar syrup (see page 73)
a dash of sparkling water

Muddle the fruit and sugar in a glass until
juicy and the sugar has dissolved. Add the
lemon juice and syrup, mix well. Add ice to
the glass and top with sparkling water.

Creamy Goats' Cheese with Roasted Tomatoes on a Crispy Spoon-shaped Cracker
MAKES 20 APPETIZERS
125 g each of goats' cheese and cream cheese
250 g sun-dried tomatoes, finely chopped
basil leaves, finely chopped, to garnish

For the crispy spoon-shaped crackers:
125 g butter
125 g plain flour
½ teaspoon salt
175 ml egg whites, about 4-5 whites
a sheet of lightweight plastic or cardboard
a sharp scalpel
a baking sheet, lightly greased

To make a spoon stencil, trace the shape of
a teaspoon on a sheet of plastic. Carefully
cut out the shape using a scalpel.

Preheat the oven to 180°C (350°F) Gas 4.
Put the butter and salt in a mixer and blend.
Gradually add the flour then slowly beat in
the egg whites. Continue to mix until the
dough is smooth. Place the stencil on a
greased baking sheet. Use a butter knife to
spread one or two tablespoons of the batter
into the stencil shape. Lift off the stencil and
repeat this process to create 10 spoon
shapes. Bake in the preheated oven for
10 minutes or until a light golden brown
on the edges. Repeat this process to make
another 10 crackers.

Put the goats' and cream cheeses in a mixer
and blend until well combined. To assemble,
top each cracker with a little goats' cheese
mixture and tomatoes. Garnish with basil.

Mushroom Consommé
SERVES 10
25 g dried cep mushrooms
1.5 litres chicken stock, warmed
450 g mushrooms, stems minced, caps sliced
3 tablespoons minced shallots
1 teaspoon salt
¼ teaspoon freshly ground black pepper
2 tablespoons dry sherry
1 tablespoon soy sauce
3 egg whites
2 egg shells, crushed
freshly squeezed lemon juice, to taste
raw enoki mushrooms, to garnish

Soak the dried mushrooms in the pot of
warmed chicken stock until soft. Discard any
hard stems and strain the stock through
muslin to remove any sand. Pour the stock
into a deep pot, add the soaked dried
mushrooms, the chopped fresh mushroom
stems, shallots, salt and pepper. Bring just
to the boil over medium heat. Reduce the
heat and simmer for 40 minutes, skimming
occasionally and keeping the level of liquid
constant by adding more water. Remove
from the heat and stir in the sherry and
soy sauce.

Beat the egg whites with the egg shells in
a large bowl. Whisking constantly, gradually
add the broth to the whites. Return to the
pot, place over medium heat, and whisk
gently until the liquid is simmering. Let
simmer for 15 minutes. The egg whites
will coagulate and float to the top, forming
a cap. Line a sieve with 2 layers of muslin
and set over large bowl. Gently ladle the
consommé into the sieve, pressing the liquid
through with the back of the ladle. Season
to taste.

Combine 750 ml water and the lemon juice
in a small saucepan and bring to the boil.
Add the sliced mushroom caps and simmer
for 2 minutes. Drain well. Transfer to a clean
stockpot and add the strained consommé.
Bring to a simmer. Ladle into bowls and
garnish with uncooked enoki mushrooms.

Chicken and Pesto Salad with Rocket
SERVES 8-10
8 chicken breasts or thighs, cooked and shredded
350 ml Pesto Vinaigrette (see page 147)
2 bunches watercress, stems removed
250 g baby rocket leaves
50 g toasted pine nuts
125 g Parmesan cheese, grated
175 g sun-dried tomatoes
sea salt and freshly ground pepper

In a large salad bowl, combine the chicken,
pesto vinaigrette, watercress and baby
rocket leaves and lightly toss. Taste and add
salt and pepper, if needed. Garnish with the
pine nuts, Parmesan cheese and sun-dried
tomatoes and serve immediately.

Note: A favourite salad with our clients – the salad will wilt quickly so be sure to combine the ingredients just as you serve the salad.

BASIC PESTO

MAKES 250 ml

125 g basil leaves
2 garlic cloves, crushed
50 g pine nuts, toasted
125 ml extra virgin olive oil
50 g grated Parmesan cheese
sea salt to taste

Combine the basil, salt, garlic and pine nuts in a food processor or blender. While the machine is running, slowly add the oil. Keep in a covered container with some extra oil on top in the refrigerator. When ready to use, add the Parmesan cheese.

PESTO VINAIGRETTE

250 ml Pesto (see recipe above)
50 ml white wine vinegar
freshly squeezed juice of 1 lemon
100 ml extra virgin olive oil
sea salt and freshly ground black pepper

In a bowl, whisk together the pesto, vinegar, lemon juice and olive oil. Season to taste with salt and pepper. The Pesto Vinaigrette is a little heavier than a usual one so use sparingly and add just before serving.

Chocolate Cupcakes

MAKES 12 CUPCAKES

85 g dark chocolate, chopped
200 g plain flour
280 g sugar
1 teaspoon bicarbonate of soda
1 teaspoon salt
250 ml soured cream or crème fraîche
6 tablespoons unsalted butter, at room temperature
2 large eggs
1½ teaspoons vanilla extract
50 ml hot coffee
Vanilla Buttercream Icing (see right)
a 12-hole cupcake tin, liberally greased
    and fitted with cupcake cases

Preheat the oven to 180°C (350°F) Gas 4. In a double boiler melt the chocolate. Remove from the heat and stir until smooth. In a separate large bowl, sift the flour, sugar, bicarbonate of soda and salt. Add the

soured cream and butter and beat for 2 minutes. Add the melted chocolate, eggs, vanilla and coffee. Beat until combined. Scrape down the bowl. Pour batter into the cupcake tins about two-thirds full. Bake in the preheated oven for 15–20 minutes or until the centre of a cake springs back when lightly pressed. Let cool in the tin for 10 minutes. Turn out and allow to cool completely before icing.

Vanilla Cupcakes

MAKES 12 CUPCAKES

175 g unsalted butter, room temperature
175 g sugar
250 g plain or cake flour
2 teaspoons baking powder
¼ teaspoon salt
6 large egg whites
175 ml milk
1 tablespoon vanilla extract
Vanilla Buttercream Icing (see below)
a 12-hole cupcake tin, liberally greased
    and fitted with cupcake cases

Preheat the oven to 180°C (350°F) Gas 4. In a large mixing bowl, beat the butter and sugar together until light and fluffy. In a separate bowl, sift together the flour, baking powder and salt. Combine the egg whites, milk and vanilla. Alternating the flour mixture and egg mixture, beginning and ending with the flour, combine into the butter and sugar mixture, scraping down the bowl frequently.

Spoon the mixture into cupcake tin and bake for 15–20 minutes, until the centre of a cake springs back when lightly pressed. Let cool in the tin for 10 minutes. Turn out and allow to cool completely before icing.

VANILLA BUTTERCREAM ICING

675 g unsalted butter, at room temperature
350 g icing sugar
2 tablespoons vanilla extract
a pinch of salt
a few drops each of red and blue food colouring

Put the butter in a bowl and slowly beat while gradually adding sugar. Scrape down the sides of the bowl and add the vanilla extract and salt. Continue to beat until the mixture is fluffy. Transfer half the icing to

a second bowl. Add blue food colouring to one and red to the other, to desired shade. Beat well. When the cupcakes are completely cooled, ice them with the Vanilla Buttercream.

Note: Coloured 'dots' may be achieved by spooning a small amount of buttercream in a piping bag fitted with a small round tip. Pipe little dots on each cupcake.

Checkerboard Cookies for a Baby Boy or Girl

MAKES 20 COOKIES

250 g unsalted butter or shortening
250 g granulated sugar
1½ teaspoons vanilla extract
280 g plain flour
2 egg (yolk only of 1)
a few drops of blue or red food colouring
50 g cocoa powder mixed with 1 tablespoon milk
    or water (needed for boy cookies only)
2 baking sheets, lightly greased or lined
    with parchment paper
4.5 cm square cookie cutter

Preheat the oven to 180°C (350°F) Gas 4. Place the butter, sugar and vanilla in a mixer or food processor and blend until smooth. Add the flour, egg and egg yolk and continue mixing until a dough just forms.

Remove half the dough. For a girl baby shower, add red food colouring to reach desired shade, leaving the second half of the dough plain. For a boy baby shower, add blue food colouring to half to reach desired shade, and with the second half, add the cocoa and milk and blend to combine.

Roll the doughs out between two sheets of parchment paper to 5 mm thickness. Cut into squares with a square cookie cutter. Arrange two squares of each colour in a checkerboard pattern (as shown opposite) on a prepared baking sheet. Bake in the preheated oven for 10–12 minutes. Remove from the oven, transfer to a wire rack and let cool completely before serving. These cookies are best eaten on the day they are baked but will keep for 2–3 days if stored in an air-tight container.

A Pink Luncheon

MENU FOR 6-8 GUESTS

APERITIF Pink Hibiscus Lemonade

BUFFET The Great Big 'Create Your Own' Salad Bar

Baby Rocket Leaves with Watercress, Mixed Baby Greens and Fresh Pea Shoots,

Marinated and Roasted Red, Yellow and Green Tomatoes

A Variety of Fresh Cherry Tomatoes and Avocado Slices

Daikon, Marinated Artichokes and Jerusalem Artichoke Crisps

Julienned Red and Yellow Peppers

Mushrooms, Edamame and Fresh Peas

Fresh Blood Orange, Pink Grapefruit and Orange Segments

Fresh Sweetcorn in a Lime Marinade

St. Agur Blue Cheese, Soft Fresh Goats' Cheese and String Cheese

Marinated Olives with Fresh Herbs

'The Kitchen's' Cheesy Croutons

A Selection of Salad Dressings including Gorgonzola, Balsamic,

Pomegranate Molasses Vinaigrette and Lemon Vinaigrette

Grilled Chicken Strips
In a Chimichuri Sauce

Italian Seafood Salad
With Lemon Vinaigrette

Edamame Rice Salad
With Wasabi Vinaigrette

DESSERT Berry Upside-Down Cake

Oeufs à la Neige

Almond Cake
With Pink Mascarpone Cream

Pretty in Pink

Decidedly feminine, pink is a perfect choice for a ladies' luncheon in this stunning rose garden at the height of its bloom. By combining mixed shades of pink, from pale to hot, in both the flowers and the food, we create a lively ambience that sets the stage for a fun, feisty party. Sitting at pink tables, starting with pink hibiscus lemonade, and ending with a variety of pink desserts, the guests at this party will bask in a blush glow from start to finish. After all, everyone looks good in pink!

Setting this party in a rose garden inevitably establishes roses as the secondary theme. Not much can compete with a perfect rose unless it's dozens upon dozens of them, so that is what we are using. We include every variety of pink rose we could find, from plump Yves Piaget garden roses to miniature spray roses, filling the table in an abundant display with dashes of lime-green viburnum and wild raspberry sprigs as fresh accents. A rose pattern adorns the antique Limoges china and a small pink rose is attached to each place card. If, as they say, pink makes one feel younger and happy, then your guests will almost certainly never want to leave.

To make the Hibiscus Concentrate, put all the ingredients in a saucepan and bring to the boil. Reduce the heat and simmer for a few minutes. Let cool and strain. The concentrate may be kept in the refrigerator for up to one week. To make the hibiscus lemonade, pour all of the ingredients into a jug. Fill the glasses with ice and pour the lemonade over. Garnish with lavender sprigs and citrus wheels.

Italian Seafood Salad
SERVES 8-10

900 g raw scallops, white parts only
900 g uncooked prawns
450 g raw squid, sliced
24 New Zealand green-lipped mussels
2 langoustines or Dublin Bay prawns
2 bunches celery, sliced crossways
250 g red and yellow cherry tomatoes, halved
1 avocado, peeled and diced into 1-cm pieces
125 ml Lemon Vinaigrette (see below)
125 g alfalfa sprouts, to garnish

For the stock:
2 unwaxed lemons, sliced
2 bay leaves
1 onion, finely chopped
250 ml dry white wine
1 tablespoon peppercorns
1 teaspoon salt
3 litres water

Lemon Vinaigrette:
100 ml freshly squeezed lemon juice
3 teaspoons honey
250 ml virgin olive oil
2 shallots, finely diced
½ teaspoon salt
½ teaspoon pepper

To make the Lemon Vinaigrette, put all the ingredients a bowl and whisk to combine. Refrigerate until ready to use.

To make the stock, put all the ingredients in a large pot and bring to the boil. Add the seafood and simmer until opaque. Remove the seafood from the stock using a slotted spoon. Transfer to a bowl, cover and set aside. Add the celery to the reserved stock and simmer for one minute. Add to the bowl of seafood and chill in the refrigerator for 1–2 hours. When ready to serve, add the

above Wild raspberries peeking out from under pink roses make this floral arrangement look good enough to eat.

Pink Hibiscus Lemonade
MAKES 4 LITRES

450 ml Hibiscus Lavender Concentrate (see below)
250–350 ml freshly squeezed lemon juice
450 g sugar
2.5 litres water
450 g crushed ice
6–8 fresh lavender sprigs, to garnish
citrus wheels, to garnish
8–10 serving glasses

Hibiscus Lavender Concentrate:
60 g dried hibiscus (dried hibiscus flowers may be found in West Indian shops or by mail order)
450 ml water
8 sprigs fresh lavender

tomatoes and avocado and lightly combine with Lemon Vinaigrette. Garnish with the alfalfa sprouts.

Grilled Chicken Strips in a Chimichuri Sauce
SERVES 8-10
6 grilled chicken breasts, cut into strips

For the Chimichuri Sauce:
125 g coarsely chopped coriander
125 g coarsely chopped parsley
60 g coarsely chopped mint
3 garlic cloves, finely chopped
4 shallots, finely chopped
125 ml red wine vinegar
a pinch of dried chilli flakes
a pinch of dried oregano
a pinch of ground cumin
125 ml olive oil
sea salt and freshly ground black pepper

To make the Chimichuri Sauce, put all the ingredients except salt and pepper in a food processor and blend until well combined. Season to taste with salt and pepper. Drizzle the chicken with the Chimichuri Sauce. Any left over will keep in an airtight container in the refrigerator for 2–3 days.

Edamame Rice Salad
SERVES 8-10
450 g long-grain rice, steamed with salt to taste
350 g cooked and shelled edamame beans
2 small cucumbers, peeled, seeded and diced
125 g finely diced celery from inner stalks
125 g thinly sliced spring onions
coarse salt
chopped mint, to taste
125 g beansprouts, if desired
2 ripe medium avocados, peeled and diced
salt and freshly ground black pepper

For the Wasabi Vinaigrette:
125 ml vegetable or sunflower oil
125 ml rice vinegar
2 teaspoons sugar
wasabi powder or paste, to taste

To make the Wasabi Vinaigrette, put the oil, vinegar and sugar in a bowl and whisk to combine. Add wasabi to taste.

Add the Wasabi Vinaigrette to the cooked and cooled rice and stir in the remaining ingredients, adding the avocados last. Season to taste with salt and pepper and serve immediately

Berry Upside-Down Cake
SERVES 8-10
125 g unsalted butter, plus 1 tablespoon melted and cooled
100 g brown sugar
450 g blackberries, raspberries, or blueberries
1 teaspoon almond extract
4 eggs, separated
125 g plain flour
1 teaspoon baking powder
¼ teaspoon salt
250 g granulated sugar
450 g fresh berries, to serve
125 g redcurrant jelly, melted (optional)
whipped cream or vanilla ice cream, to serve
a 25 cm circular baking tin, with 6 cm sides

Preheat the oven to 180°C (350°F) Gas 4. Put the 100g butter in the baking tin. Put it in the oven to melt the butter. Remove from the oven, swirl to coat the tin evenly and add the brown sugar. Stir and return to the oven for 5 minutes, stirring once or twice, then remove. Spread the berries in a single layer on the sugar.

Whisk the melted butter and almond extract into the egg yolks and set aside. In another bowl, sift together the flour, baking powder and salt. Beat the egg whites on medium speed until they form soft peaks. Do not overbeat. Fold the granulated sugar into the egg whites quarter at a time. Then fold in the egg yolk mixture quarter at a time. Finally, fold in the flour mixture quarter at a time. Pour this batter over the berries and spread evenly to form a smooth surface.

Bake for about 30 minutes. A skewer inserted in the centre of the cake should come out clean when it is ready. Let stand for at least 10 minutes before unmoulding. Add the additional fresh berries to the cake before serving. Glaze them with the melted redcurrant jelly, if using. Serve with whipped cream or vanilla ice cream.

Oeufs à la Neige

SERVES 6-8

4 large egg whites, at room temperature

1 teaspoon vanilla extract

¼ teaspoon cream of tartar

¼ teaspoon salt

150 g caster sugar

450 g fresh red berries of your choice

For the Raspberry Crème Anglaise:

6 egg yolks

150 g sugar

300 ml hot milk

1 tablespoon vanilla extract

3 tablespoons unsalted butter

100 g raspberries, puréed

a 30 x 30 cm baking tin

6–8 large Martini glasses or similar

Preheat the oven to 190°C (375°F) Gas 5. Beat the egg whites until foamy. Add the vanilla, cream of tartar and salt, and beat until soft peaks form. Gradually beat in the sugar. Increase the speed to high and beat until thick and glossy peaks form. Transfer the mixture to the baking tin. Bake in the preheated oven for 10–15 minutes, until golden brown.

Meanwhile, make the Raspberry Crème Anglaise. Over a double boiler, whisk the egg yolks, adding the sugar gradually until the mixture is fluffy and pale yellow. Whisk in the milk and vanilla. Remove from the heat and whisk in the butter. Let cool and fold in the raspberry purée.

Spoon some Raspberry Crème Anglaise into each serving dish. Top with a large scoop of meringue and garnish with fresh berries.

Almond Cake with Pink Mascarpone Cream

MAKES 1 LARGE CAKE

250 g ready-made almond paste

125 g unsalted butter, softened

125 g sugar

3 eggs

2 teaspoons finely grated lemon zest

2 tablespoons Grand Marnier, or Amaretto

60 g plain flour

½ teaspoon baking powder

balsamic-marinated strawberries and candied orange peel, to garnish (optional)

an 20 cm round cake tin, lightly buttered and floured

For the Pink Mascarpone Cream:

450 g mascarpone cheese

3 tablespoons sugar

125 ml Grand Marnier

100 g raspberries, puréed

2 teaspoons grated orange zest

450 ml whipped cream

Preheat the oven to 180°C (350°F) Gas 4. To make the cake, put the almond paste, butter and sugar in a bowl and mix. One at a time, beat in the eggs, followed by the lemon zest and Grand Marnier. Sift the flour and baking powder together, and add to the almond mixture until just combined. Pour this batter into the prepared cake tin and bake in the preheated oven for 35–40 minutes, until a toothpick inserted in the centre of the cake comes out clean. Let cool on a rack before removing the cake from the tin.

To make the Mascarpone Cream, beat together the mascarpone, sugar, Grand Marnier, puréed raspberries, and orange zest until well combined and fluffy. Fold in the whipped cream. When ready to serve, spoon onto slices of the cake and garnish with strawberries and candied orange peel.

A Moroccan-style Party

MENU FOR 8-10

APERITIF   Orange Blossom Cocktail

TO BE PASSED   Moroccan Savoury Stars
With a Fresh Tomato Chutney

FAMILY STYLE   Baked Aubergines with Chermoula Sauce

Fruity Chicken Tagine

Beetroot and Melon Salad
With a Citrus Vinaigrette

Moroccan-style Carrots

Roasted Herb-filled Leg of Lamb
With a Fresh Mint Pistou

Wedding Rice

DESSERT   Fromage Blanc with Figs
With Honey and Toasted Almonds

'Mark's Garden designed gorgeous arrangements of orange roses that
I used throughout my film "Hanging up" to perfectly accent the mood
of various scenes.'

Diane Keaton

Casablanca Revisited

Come with us to the casbah. Not everyone is lucky enough to be able to throw a Moroccan party in an authentic-looking pavilion such as this one we found on the former estate of set designer Tony Duquette. But we were and it became a fantastic inspiration. We wanted to create the same sense of mystery and romance that not only was depicted in legendary films of the past but actually still exists in nooks and crannies off the convoluted streets of Moroccan cities today. Our further aim was to capture a little of the magic of the place that has sparked artists like Delacroix and Matisse and create an artistic environment of our own.

In selecting our colour palette, we were further influenced by the colourful food on our menu and the wide array of the traditional spices used in this cuisine. Dominating the main table are tall, vividly coloured spires of pavéd fruit combined with traditional flowers. Included are dried dates, figs, apricots, peaches and papaya, alternated with small yellow chrysanthemums and cymbidium orchids. A collage of spicy red, orange and yellow tones is mixed with earthy browns and touches of vivid blue. With the family-style setup and the abundance of food, our setting spills over to side tables and even to the floor that we cover with multi-coloured rose petals and tea lights. We have hung strands of orchid blossoms from the arches in the background and tucked marigolds among the heaping dishes of food. An antique brass coffee urn serves as a vase for exotic flowering vines. Traditional Moroccan tea glasses are used for drinking as well as votive candles which will burn late into the night if this party is anything like the ones that take place in Tangier. All in all it becomes an incredible banquet for the eyes and the soul as much as the stomach.

Orange Blossom Cocktail

MAKES 1 DRINK

400 ml orange-infused vodka
a splash of freshly squeezed lemon juice
a splash of freshly squeezed orange juice
1–2 drops orange blossom water
40 ml apricot nectar
50 ml unfiltered apple juice
slice of orange, to garnish

Put all the ingredients in a shaker filled with ice and shake. Pour into a Moroccan tea glass or tumbler to serve.

Moroccan Savoury Stars

MAKES 36–48 STARS

450 g quick-cooking polenta
vegetable oil, for frying
250 g mild goats' cheese, at room temperature
250 g cream cheese, at room temperature
450 g Fresh Tomato Chutney (see below)
mint leaves, to garnish
a baking tray with sides, greased
a star cookie cutter

Cook the polenta according to the packet directions. Spread onto the prepared baking tray and leave to cool. Cut into small stars. In a large, deep frying pan, heat 3–5 cm of oil to 130°C. Fry the polenta stars until they are pale golden brown and crisp. This may be done in advance and the stars reheated for a few minutes in a preheated 190°C (375°F) Gas 5 oven.

Put the goats' cheese and cream cheese in a bowl and blend. Top each warm star with 1 teaspoon cheese mixture and 1 teaspoon tomato chutney. Garnish with a mint leaf.

FRESH TOMATO CHUTNEY

MAKES 2 LITRES

125 g fresh ginger, peeled and chopped
250 ml cider vinegar
450 g brown sugar
450 g granulated sugar
2 lemons, sliced
1 tablespoon ground cinnamon
1 tablespoon ground cumin
½ teaspoon ground cloves
¼ teaspoon freshly ground black pepper
1 teaspoon sea salt
450 g each yellow and red cherry tomatoes, halved
125 g mint leaves, finely chopped

Put the first 10 ingredients in a pan with 250 ml water. Bring to the boil, reduce the heat and simmer until slightly thickened, stirring occasionally. Remove from the heat and strain. Add the tomatoes and mint.

The chutney may be made ahead of time and refrigerated for up to 2 days. Any extra chutney is a good topping for grilled chicken breast or fish fillet.

Baked Aubergines with Chermoula Sauce

SERVES 8–10

6–8 small long aubergines, trimmed and cut lengthways
3–4 red peppers, deseeded and quartered
olive oil, for brushing
30 g chopped thyme
200 ml Chermoula Sauce (see below)
125 g roasted and salted Spanish Marcona almonds
mint leaves, torn
sea salt and freshly ground black pepper
a baking tray, lined with greaseproof paper

Preheat the oven to 190°C (375°F) Gas 5. Put the aubergines and peppers on the lined baking tray. Brush with olive oil, sprinkle with thyme and season with salt and pepper. Bake in the preheated oven for 25–30 minutes, or until the aubergines are tender. Arrange on a warmed platter and drizzle with Chermoula Sauce. Scatter the almonds and mint leaves over the top to garnish. Serve warm or at room temperature.

CHERMOULA SAUCE

MAKES ABOUT 250 ML

1 onion, chopped
6 garlic cloves, chopped
2 teaspoons ground cumin
1 teaspoon paprika
½ teaspoon saffron threads, crushed and steeped in 2 tablespoons hot water
50 g flat leaf parsley
50 g coriander
6 tablespoons olive oil
6 tablespoons freshly squeezed lemon juice
sea salt and freshly ground black pepper

Put all the ingredients in a food processor and blend to combine. Serve the sauce at room temperature. Any left over can be stored for 2–3 days in the refrigerator.

Fruity Chicken Tagine

SERVES 8–10

2 teaspoons ground cinnamon
2 teaspoons ground ginger
2 teaspoons turmeric
2 pinches of saffron threads
1 teaspoon sea salt
1 teaspoon freshly ground black pepper
125 g butter or 125 ml vegetable oil
8 chicken breasts, bone-in
4 chicken thighs, bone-in
3-4 onions, chopped
2-3 garlic cloves, peeled and crushed
450–500 ml chicken stock or water
450 g dried apricots, sliced
450 g dates or prunes, stoned and sliced
250 g salted and roasted Spanish Marcona almonds
cinnamon sticks and coriander sprigs, to garnish
a tagine (optional)

Combine the cinnamon, ginger, turmeric, saffron, salt and pepper in a bowl. Rub the chicken pieces with the spice mixture.

Melt the butter in a large pot or tagine with lid. Sauté the chicken pieces until browned. Add the onions and garlic and cook for another 5 minutes. Cover with chicken stock or water. Bring the mixture to a full boil, then reduce the heat to a low simmer. Cover and cook for about 30 minutes, until the chicken is tender. Remove the chicken from the pot, bone it, and pull into medium-sized pieces. Return it to the pot and add the apricots and dates. Simmer for another 10 minutes. Add the almonds and serve garnished with cinnamon sticks and coriander sprigs.

Beetroot and Melon Salad

SERVES 8–10

5 yellow beetroot, cooked and peeled
1 cantaloupe melon, peeled and deseeded
150 g alfalfa or other sprouted seeds
75 ml Citrus Vinaigrette (see right)
125 g soft goats' cheese
sea salt and freshly ground black pepper

Slice or julienne the beetroot and cantaloupe, as similar in size as possible. On a platter, alternate beetroot and cantaloupe. Arrange the alfalfa along the centre, drizzle with Citrus Vinaigrette and season with salt and pepper. Crumble or scatter the cheese over the top and serve at room temperature.

CITRUS VINAIGRETTE

the zest and freshly squeezed juice of 1 lemon,
    1 lime and 1 orange
175 ml olive oil
sea salt and freshly ground black pepper

Whisk together the zest and juice of all the fruits. Slowly whisk in the olive oil. Season to taste with salt and pepper, and sharpen with more juice, if needed.

Moroccan-style Carrots

SERVES 8–10

8-10 baby or young carrots, topped, tailed
    and peeled
1½ teaspoons ground cumin
1 teaspoon ground cinnamon
1 teaspoon ground ginger
2 teaspoons grated fresh ginger
dash of Tabasco or dried chilli flakes
3 tablespoons freshly squeezed orange juice
125 ml olive oil
60 g mint, finely chopped
sea salt and freshly ground black pepper

Steam or boil the carrots in salted water until tender. Drain and dust with cumin, cinnamon, ground and fresh ginger, Tabasco and lemon juice. Stir to coat well and marinate for at least an hour. Heat the oil in a large frying pan over medium-high heat. Add the carrots, heat through and season to taste with salt and pepper. Garnish with mint and serve.

Roasted Herb-Filled Leg of Lamb

SERVES 8–10

a 2.25-2.7 kg leg of lamb, boned and butterflied
3 tablespoons olive oil
2 garlic cloves, peeled and crushed
30 g chopped rosemary
30 g chopped thyme
Fresh Mint Pistou, to serve (see page 25)
sea salt and freshly ground black pepper
kitchen string

Preheat the oven to 230°C (450°F) Gas 8. Trim the lamb of excess fat and flatten it as evenly as possible. Brush the lamb with olive oil and spread the garlic, rosemary and thyme over it. Season with salt and pepper. Roll up the lamb lengthways and tie securely at 5-cm intervals with kitchen string.

Put the lamb in a shallow roasting tin. For medium rare, roast until a thermometer inserted in the meat shows 52°C, about 45 minutes. Leave to rest for 10 minutes. Slice and serve with Fresh Mint Pistou.

Wedding Rice

SERVES 8–10

750 g long grain rice
1 litre chicken stock or water
1½ teaspoons sea salt
½ teaspoon saffron threads

Fruit and nut topping:
50 g butter
75 g Spanish Marcona almonds or pine nuts
100 g dried apricots, sliced
100 g dates, stoned and sliced
100 g dried cranberries
100 g sultanas
50 g currants
250 g pomegranate seeds (optional)

Put the rice, stock, salt and saffron in a medium pan and bring to the boil. Reduce the heat, cover and cook for 15 minutes until the liquid is absorbed and the rice tender.

To make the topping, melt the butter in a large frying pan. Add the almonds and fry, stirring, until lightly browned. Add the remaining ingredients and cook until heated through. Stir often as this burns easily.

When ready to serve, turn the rice out onto a large heated platter and cover with topping.

Fromage Blanc with Figs

SERVES 8–10

450 ml fromage blanc
250 ml crème fraîche or soured cream
2 egg whites
125 g granulated sugar
1 teaspoon almond extract or Amaretto
honey, to drizzle
fresh figs and toasted flaked almonds, to serve

In a mixing bowl, combine the fromage blanc and crème fraîche. Beat the egg whites until soft peaks form, gradually adding the sugar. Fold the egg whites into the cheese mixture, then add the almond extract. Drizzle with honey and serve with figs and almonds.

50s Retro Party

MENU FOR 8–10 GUESTS

APERITIF   Brent's Manhattan

BUFFET   Grilled Vegetables

With Herb Marinade and Toasted Breadcrumb Topping

Individual Meat Loaves

Rigatoni and Gruyère 'Mac and Cheese'

With White Truffle Oil

Build-Your-Own Cobb Salad Bar

With Blue Cheese Dressing and Creamy Parmesan Dressing

Baked Potato Bar

With a Selection of Savoury Toppings

DESSERT   Cupcake and Candy Bar

Chocolate Cupcakes with Chocolate Sour Cream Icing

Orange Butter Cupcakes with Cream Cheese Coconut Frosting

Red Velvet Cupcakes

A Selection of Popular Retro Confectionery

Rock and Roll

Food from the 1950s has become the classic American food and its appeal is widespread. There is something about the simplicity of the 1950s itself that still evokes a happy feeling. Along with our inviting array of mouthwatering foods, we wanted to create an ambience that also evoked those happy days. This demands bright joyful flowers and nothing surpasses gerberas in this department.

Zany and madcap are good terms for the pavéd gerbera daisy heads covering the counters of this 50s-inspired kitchen. We like the 'technicolour' image this table presents with the gradation of hot-toned flower heads weaving around and about the overflowing platters. The tall floral display of gerberas lined with stripes of pavéd button mums strikes just the right impudent pose for this casual tongue-in-cheek presentation.

above Bands of button mums surround the edges of the glass containers filled with popular sweets of the period, like jellybeans, wine gums and liquorice.

Brent's Manhattan
MAKES 1 DRINK
150 ml Maker's Mark bourbon
25 ml French Dry Vermouth
25 ml Italian Sweet Vermouth
4 dashes of orange bitters
1–2 dashes of Angostura bitters
a splash of syrup from a jar of Morello cherries
a cherry, such as Morello, Amarena, Maraschino
    or bing, to garnish

Pour the ingredients into an ice-filled mixing glass or Martini pitcher. Stir, do not shake, until well chilled. Strain into a chilled cocktail glass. Garnish with a cherry and serve.

Grilled Vegetables with Herb Marinade and Toasted Breadcrumb Topping
SERVES 8–10
6 red, yellow or orange peppers, stemmed
    and cut into quarters
4 carrots, tipped, steamed and sliced
3–4 red onions, trimmed and cut into
    2.5-cm wedges
4 baby aubergines, trimmed and sliced
2 fennel bulbs, trimmed and cut vertically into
    2.5-cm wedges
4–5 green and yellow courgettes, sliced

For the herb marinade:
60 ml olive oil
2 garlic cloves, minced
2 tablespoons chopped parsley
2 tablespoons chopped basil
2 tablespoons chopped sage

For the breadcrumb topping:
45 g butter
2–3 garlic cloves, minced
1–2 teaspoons dried chilli flakes, to taste
1 tablespoon chopped parsley
250 g Japanese Panko or other dry breadcrumbs
sea salt and freshly ground black pepper
a charcoal or gas barbecue

To make the marinade, put all of the ingredients in small bowl and whisk to combine. Cover and chill until ready to use.

To make the topping, melt the butter in a frying pan over medium heat, add the garlic and gently sauté. Add the chilli flakes, parsley and breadcrumbs. Stir continuously until golden. Season with salt and pepper. Start the charcoal or gas barbecue and bring to medium/high heat. Brush the vegetables with the herb marinade. Grill them, turning often, until charred and tender. Arrange the vegetables on a platter and sprinkle with toasted breadcrumbs.

Individual Meat Loaves
MAKES 12–15 MINI LOAVES
3 tablespoons butter or olive oil
2 large onions, chopped
2 garlic cloves, finely chopped
1.3 kg lean minced beef
225 g passata or chopped tinned tomatoes
2 eggs, lightly beaten
125 g soft bread crumbs
2 tablespoons brown sauce
50 g Cheddar or Parmesan cheese, grated
250 ml tomato ketchup
sea salt and freshly ground black pepper
12–15 mini-loaf tins or muffin tins, oiled

Preheat the oven to 180°C (350°F) Gas 4. Melt the butter in a frying pan over medium low heat. Add the onion and garlic and cook for about 5 minutes, until soft. Put the cooled onion and garlic mixture in a large bowl and add all the remaining ingredients, except the ketchup, and mix.

Divide the meat loaf mixture between the mini-loaf tins or muffin tins. Brush each meat loaf with 1 tablespoon of ketchup. Bake in the preheated oven for 20–25 minutes, until browned and cooked through.

Note: The Meat Loaves can be made ahead of time. Let cool and freeze on a baking tray, then package in freezer bags. When ready to serve, defrost and reheat in a 180°C (350°F) Gas 4 oven for 15–20 minutes.

Rigatoni and Gruyère 'Mac and Cheese' with White Truffle Oil
SERVES 8–10
675 g rigatoni or other tube pasta
115 g unsalted butter
50 g plain flour
700 ml single cream or whole milk
250 g Gruyère cheese
white truffle oil, to taste
250 g breadcrumbs, tossed in 25 g melted butter
sea salt and freshly ground black pepper
a large baking dish or gratin, buttered

Preheat oven to 200°C (400°F) Gas 6. Bring a large saucepan of water to the boil, add a couple of pinches of salt and add the pasta. Cook the pasta until just tender. Drain, rinse and place in a large mixing bowl.

Melt the butter in a saucepan. Beat in the flour and cook until lightly browned, about 5 minutes. Add the cream or milk and continue to beat and cook until the mixture thickens and is smooth. Add the cheese, continue to beat, and add white truffle oil and salt and pepper to taste. Pour the sauce over the pasta and mix well. Taste, adding more white truffle oil and/or salt and pepper if necessary. Pour into the prepared baking dish. Top with the buttered breadcrumbs.

Bake in the preheated oven for 15–20 minutes, until heated through and browned on top. Let sit for 5 minutes before serving.

Build-Your-Own Cobb Salad Bar
SERVES 8–10
1–2 heads iceberg lettuce
1 bunch watercress
1 head Cos lettuce
Condiments:
4–5 tomatoes, chopped
250 g smoked streaky bacon, fried and chopped
5 hard-boiled eggs, chopped or sliced
450 g ham, sliced into strips
4 celery stalks, chopped
700 g cooked, shelled prawns, dressed in 50 ml
    olive oil and freshly squeezed juice of 1 lemon
750 g grilled chicken breast, sliced
200 g black olives, drained
2 red and yellow peppers, deseeded and sliced
250 g Cheddar cheese, coarsely grated
2 avocados, peeled, stoned and sliced
250 g blue cheese, crumbled
1 bunch red radishes, sliced
250 g croutons
sea salt and freshly ground black pepper
Blue Cheese Dressing or Creamy Parmesan
    Dressing, to serve (see page 170)

Chop the iceberg, watercress and romaine lettuces. Place them in a large salad bowl.

Surround with bowls of the condiments. Put the Blue Cheese Dressing and Creamy Parmesan Dressing in jugs. Let your guests place lettuce on plates and top with their choice of condiments and salad dressing. Alternately, arrange the greens in a large shallow salad bowl, season with salt and pepper, then arrange the condiments in rows on top of the greens.

BLUE CHEESE DRESSING
MAKES 450 ML
125 g blue cheese, crumbled
50 ml hot water
120 ml soured cream or Greek yoghurt
120 ml good-quality mayonnaise
freshly squeezed juice from ½ lemon
1 tablespoon Worcestershire sauce
2 garlic cloves, mashed in 1 teaspoon salt
freshly ground black pepper

Place the crumbled blue cheese in a bowl. Pour hot water over the cheese and mash with a fork. Add the remaining ingredients and mix well. Season to taste with pepper. The dressing will keep in an airtight jar in the refrigerator for 2–3 days.

CREAMY PARMESAN DRESSING
MAKES 450 ML
2 tablespoons freshly squeezed lemon juice
2 tablespoons white balsamic vinegar
2 garlic cloves, chopped
1 shallot, finely chopped
1 egg
3–4 dashes of Tabasco or other hot sauce, to taste
250 ml olive oil
125 g grated Parmesan cheese
sea salt and freshly ground black pepper

Put the lemon juice, vinegar, garlic, shallot, egg and Tabasco in a blender. With the machine running, pour in the oil in a slow and steady stream until thickened. Add the Parmesan cheese. Season to taste with salt and pepper. The dressing will keep in an airtight jar in the refrigerator for 2–3 days

Baked Potato Bar
SERVES 8-10
5 King Edward or other large baking potatoes
5 sweet potatoes
butter or olive oil, for rubbing

Potato toppings:
grated Cheshire and Cheddar cheeses
Parmesan cheese shavings
smoked bacon rashers, fried and chopped
finely sliced spring onions
crispy-fried leeks
soured cream or crème fraîche
a selection of ready-made herb-flavoured butters

Preheat the oven to 180°C (350°F) Gas 4. Scrub and trim the potatoes. Pierce each one with a skewer or sharp knife. Rub with butter or olive oil. Place on a baking tray and bake in the preheated oven for 1–1½ hours. Test with a fork for doneness. When ready to serve, slice accordion-style and place on a warmed platter. Put the toppings in attractive bowls and arrange them around the platter of potatoes. Let your guests help themselves and top their own potatoes with the fillings of their choice.

Cupcake and Candy Bar
Bake a variety of cupcakes and buy fruit jams, syrups, chocolate sauce, caramel sauce and a variety of small retro sweets and sprinkles. Gather together a selection of empty tins and jars and make sure they are very clean. You will also need silicone pastry brushes and coloured craft paper. Wrap the containers with paper and fill them with the toppings. Guests are invited to choose their cupcake and use the brushes to add decoration to their cake. They can drizzle with sauces and syrups and add sweets to create their own unique design!

Chocolate Cupcakes with Chocolate Sour Cream Icing
MAKES 24 CUPCAKES
250 g plain flour
175 g unsweetened cocoa powder
1½ teaspoons bicarbonate of soda
¼ teaspoon baking powder
¼ teaspoon salt
3 large eggs
325 g granulated sugar
1½ teaspoons vanilla extract
250 ml good-quality mayonnaise
325 ml warm water
1 quantity Chocolate Sour Cream Icing (see right)
2 x 12-hole muffin tin, liberally buttered and lined with cupcake cases

Preheat the oven to 180°C (350°F) Gas 4. Sift the flour, cocoa, bicarbonate of soda, baking powder and salt into a large bowl. In a separate bowl, beat the eggs, sugar and vanilla until pale yellow. Reduce to a lower speed and beat in the mayonnaise. Add the flour mixture alternately with the water into the egg and sugar mixture, beginning and ending with the flour mixture. Pour into the prepared muffin tins and bake in the preheated oven for about 20 minutes, or until the centre of a cake springs back when lightly pressed. Remove from the oven, let cool for about 10 minutes, then transfer to a wire rack to cool. When completely cool, frost the cakes with Chocolate Sour Cream Icing, or topping of your choice.

CHOCOLATE SOUR CREAM ICING
100 g bitter dark chocolate
2 tablespoons unsalted butter
175 ml sour cream
1 teaspoon vanilla extract
350–400 g sifted icing sugar
2 tablespoons Kahlúa (optional)

Melt the chocolate and butter in a double boiler. In a mixing bowl, beat together the sour cream and vanilla. Gradually add the icing sugar. Add the chocolate mixture and beat until smooth. Add Kahlúa, if using, and mix well to combine. Use to top Chocolate Cupcakes (see left).

Orange Butter Cupcakes with Cream Cheese Coconut Frosting
MAKES 24 CUPCAKES
250 g plain flour
2½ teaspoons baking powder
¼ teaspoon salt
280 g unsalted butter, softened
280 g granulated sugar
4 eggs
1 tablespoon finely grated orange zest
50 ml freshly squeezed orange juice, strained
125 ml whole milk
1 quantity Cream Cheese Coconut Frosting (see right)
2 x 12-hole muffin tins, liberally buttered and lined with cupcake cases

Preheat the oven to 180°C (350°F) Gas 4. Sift the flour, baking powder and salt into a large bowl. Put the butter and sugar in a separate bowl and cream until smooth, gradually beat in the eggs and add the orange zest. Mix the orange juice and milk together. Add the flour mixture alternately

with the milk and orange juice mixture, into the butter, egg and sugar mixture, ending with the flour mixture.

Pour the mixture into the prepared muffin tins and bake in the preheated oven for about 20 minutes, or until the centre of a cake springs back when lightly pressed. Remove from the oven, let cool for about 10 minutes, then transfer to a wire rack to cool. When completely cool, frost the cakes with Cream Cheese Coconut Frosting, or topping of your choice.

CREAM CHEESE COCONUT FROSTING
450 g cream cheese, at room temperature
125 g unsalted butter, at room temperature
50 ml tinned sweetened cream of coconut
50 ml double cream
1 teaspoon coconut flavouring or vanilla extract
250–300 g icing sugar
125 g sweetened, shredded coconut

Put the cream cheese and butter in a bowl and beat until smooth. Add the cream of coconut, cream and your choice of flavouring. Beat well. Gradually add the icing sugar until you have your desired consistency. Use to top Orange Butter Cupcakes (see left).

Red Velvet Cupcakes
MAKES 24 CUPCAKES
250 g plain flour
3 tablespoons unsweetened cocoa powder
½ teaspoon sea salt
1 teaspoon bicarbonate of soda
125 g unsalted butter, softened
350 g granulated sugar
2 eggs
250 ml buttermilk or whole milk
1 teaspoon vanilla extract
50 ml red food colouring
1 tablespoon white vinegar
1 quantity Vanilla Buttercream Frosting (see page 147)
2 x 12-hole muffin tin, liberally buttered and lined with cupcake cases

Preheat the oven to 180°C (350°F) Gas 4. Sift the flour, cocoa, salt and bicarbonate of soda into a large bowl. Put the butter and sugar in a separate bowl and beat until light and fluffy. Add the eggs to the butter and sugar mixture and continue to beat well. Add the flour and cocoa mixture to the egg and sugar mixture, alternately with the buttermilk, beginning and ending with the flour mixture. Beat in the vanilla and fold in the red food colouring and vinegar.

Pour the mixture into the prepared muffin pans and bake in the preheated oven for about 20 minutes, or until the centre of a cake springs back when lightly pressed.

Remove from the oven, let cool for about 10 minutes, then transfer to a wire rack to cool. When completely cool, frost the cakes with Vanilla Buttercream Frosting, or topping of your choice.

Caribbean Mood Dinner

MENU FOR 8–10 GUESTS

APERITIF — Mojito

TO BE PASSED — Jerk Chicken
On a Banana Leaf with a Mango Salsa

BUFFET — Beef Satays
With a Black Bean Sauce

'Moros y Cristianos'
Black Beans, Tomatoes and Steamed White Rice

Garden Green Salad
With a Passion Fruit Vinaigrette and Lotus Crisps

Island Sweet Bread

DESSERT — Fresh Pineapple Flambé
Served over Vanilla Ice Cream, in a Lace Cookie Cup with Sesame Seeds

Passion Fruit Crème Brûlée

below A crystal girandole is given
a Caribbean flair with pineapples,
some clam shells, sea fans, beads
and a few stems of luscious orchids.

Calypso Kick

The Caribbean is one of the great holiday playgrounds. Delicious food and sandy beaches are such a big part of the enjoyment of the inhabitants of those tropical isles that we were inspired to incorporate those elements into our décor. The hot spicy colours we've adopted, including reds, oranges and yellows mixed with sexy pinks and purples, reflect their tasty cuisine and their zest for life against a backdrop of lush tropical greenery. This décor definitely says 'Let's have a party!'

Succulent tropical fruit is incorporated with brilliant exotic flowers in the centre of this table to create an unusual architectural centrepiece. Bright orange bird of paradise blooms are packed into crystal bowls lined with tropical leaves and surrounded with purple orchids and hot pink cockscomb. The fruit is stacked alternately between the floral pieces and some of the melons are sliced open to display splashes of the vivid colours of their interior. Orange clam shells and Kukui beads are added so the entire centrepiece spills across the table in a loose casual manner, with taper candles in gold candleholders and a miniature pineapple on its stem placed on each napkin to complete the eclectic playfulness of the Caribbean style.

Mojito

MAKES 1 DRINK

1 lime, sliced into wedges
2 heaped teaspoons brown sugar
1 small handful mint leaves
30 ml white rum
a splash of soda water, to taste
15 ml Meyer's Rum (dark)
mint sprig, to garnish
a muddler

Put all but 1 of the lime wedges and all the brown sugar and mint into a rocks glass and muddle well. Fill the glass with ice and add the white rum and soda water to taste. Pour in the Meyer's rum over the back of a spoon. Finish with a lime wedge and a sprig of mint.

Beef Satays

SERVES 8–10

250 ml soy sauce
250 ml pineapple juice
½ yellow onion, finely chopped
60 g sugar
65 ml Sambal or other hot chilli sauce
1 jalapeño, seeds and vein removed, finely chopped
1 teaspoon ground nutmeg
1 tablespoon ground cinnamon
500–700 g beefsteak, cut into thin strips
36–48 white pearl onions
black bean sauce, to serve (see below)
sea salt and freshly ground black pepper
18–24 wood or metal skewers

Combine the first 8 ingredients and season to taste with salt and pepper. Skewer the beef strips and onions and marinate them in the mixture for at least 2 hours or overnight. Barbecue over a medium flame and serve immediately with Black Bean Sauce.

Note: At The Kitchen we use skirt steak or flap beef. Any tender steak will work well.

BLACK BEAN SAUCE

MAKES ABOUT 900 ML

3 tablespoons vegetable oil
2 garlic cloves, crushed
2 tablespoons grated fresh ginger
½ red onion, medium diced

500 g tinned black beans, drained
60 g fermented black beans, soaked, rinsed and coarsely chopped
1 each red, yellow and green pepper, deseeded and medium diced
30 ml white wine
1 jalapeño, deseeded and finely chopped
450 g tinned pineapple cubes
250 g peeled, stoned and cubed mango
2 tablespoons light brown sugar
2–3 teaspoons mild curry powder
2 tablespoons freshly squeezed lime juice
3 spring onions, sliced
2 tablespoons chopped coriander
sea salt
chicken stock, for thinning (optional)

Heat the oil in a large frying pan over medium heat. Add the garlic and ginger and when just fragrant add the onion and sauté for 1 minute. Add the remaining ingredients except the lime juice, spring onions and coriander. Bring to a simmer. Remove from the heat and stir in the lime juice, spring onions and coriander. Add salt to taste and a little chicken stock if the sauce is too thick.

Jerk Chicken

MAKES 15–20 APPETIZERS

1 tablespoon whole allspice
1 tablespoon black peppercorns
1 small cinnamon stick
2 cloves
1 teaspoon ground nutmeg
2 medium onions, coarsely chopped
4 spring onions, chopped
½ Scotch bonnet or habanero chilli, deseeded and chopped
4 cloves garlic, coarsely chopped
a 2.5-cm piece fresh ginger, peeled and sliced
125 ml tamarind paste
125 g brown sugar
freshly squeezed juice of 2 limes
65 ml extra virgin olive oil
3 chicken breasts, washed and dried
65 ml Chipotle Sauce, plus extra if needed (see recipe on page 105)
coriander sprigs, to garnish
mango salsa, to serve (see right)

cool, shred the meat, and put it in a large bowl. Add the chipotle sauce and stir. Season and set aside.

To make the tostones, heat some oil to 180°C in a deep heavy frying pan or wok. Peel the plantains and slice thinly using a mandoline. Fry the slices to a light golden brown and drain on kitchen paper. Sprinkle with sea salt flakes.

MANGO SALSA
2 ripe mangos, peeled, stoned and finely diced
1 red pepper, deseeded and finely diced
1 small red onion, finely chopped
1 tablespoon finely diced jalapeno chilli
1½ teaspoons crushed garlic
180 ml rice wine vinegar
a small handful of coriander, finely chopped
sea salt and freshly ground black pepper

Put all the ingredients in a bowl and stir to combine. Season to taste with salt and pepper. Chill until ready to serve.

To assemble, put a large tablespoon of jerk chicken on the end of each tostone. Top with Mango Salsa and garnish with coriander.

Moros y Cristianos
SERVES 8-10
2 tablespoons extra virgin olive oil
1 medium onion, finely chopped
1 tablespoon crushed garlic
750 g tinned black beans, drained
250 g chopped fresh tomatoes
250 ml chicken or vegetable stock
750 g Steamed White Rice (see below)
sea salt and freshly ground black pepper

Put the oil in a large, deep frying pan over medium heat. Add the onion, season and cook until soft, about 4−5 minutes. Stir in the garlic, beans, tomatoes and stock. Turn the heat to medium/high and cook, stirring, for about 7−8 minutes, or until the beans are hot and most of the liquid is evaporated. To serve, put the hot white rice on a platter and top with the black bean mixture.

STEAMED WHITE RICE
1.2 litres water, chicken stock or vegetable stock
450 g long grain rice
2 teaspoons sea salt

Put the water, rice and salt in a large pan and bring to the boil. Cover and reduce the heat. Simmer until all the liquid is absorbed and the rice is tender, about 20 minutes.

Garden Green Salad with Passion Fruit Vinaigrette
SERVES 8-10
8 handfuls mixed baby leaf salad
2 mangos, peeled, stoned and cut into bite-sized cubes
1 pineapple, peeled, cored and cut into bite-sized cubes
2 papayas, peeled, deseeded and cut into bite-sized cubes
6 kiwis, peeled and sliced
2 avocados, peeled, stoned and sliced
sea salt and freshly ground black pepper

PASSION FRUIT VINAIGRETTE
65 ml ready-made passion fruit purée
65 ml freshly squeezed lemon juice
100 ml extra virgin olive oil
sea salt and freshly ground black pepper

LOTUS CRISPS
corn or vegetable oil, for frying
2 lotus fruits

To make the vinaigrette, put the passion fruit purée and lemon juice in a bowl and whisk to combine. While whisking, slowly add in the olive oil. Season to taste with salt and pepper.

To make the lotus crisps, heat the oil to 180°C in a heavy, deep frying pan. Thinly slice the lotus on a mandoline. Fry in oil until golden brown and drain on kitchen paper.

To assemble the salad, put the greens in a large bowl. Season with salt and pepper and toss with some of the Passion Fruit Vinaigrette. Mound the greens on a serving

PLANTAIN TOSTONE
corn or vegetable oil, for frying
2-3 plantains, yellow or green, not dark and ripe
sea salt flakes

In a sauté pan over medium heat, add the allspice, peppercorns, cinnamon stick, cloves and nutmeg. Toast for 1−2 minutes, but do not allow them to burn. Put in a clean coffee or spice grinder and process to a powder. Put the remaining ingredients, except for the chicken and chipotle sauce, in a food processor or blender, add the spice mix, and purée until smooth. Add more oil if needed and season with salt and pepper.

Put the chicken breasts in a ziplock bag, add the jerk spice mixture and marinate in the refrigerator for at least 2 hours or overnight if possible.

Preheat the oven to 180°C (350°F) Gas 4. Put the chicken in a roasting tin and bake in the preheated oven for 20−25 minutes or until cooked through. Once the chicken is platter. Surround with the fruit. Drizzle more Passion Fruit Vinaigrette over the fruit and top with sliced avocado and lotus crisps.

Island Sweet Bread

MAKES 1 LOAF

2 tablespoons instant dried yeast
60 g instant potato flakes
150 g sugar
125 g butter
60 g powdered milk
3 eggs
1 teaspoon salt
½ teaspoon vanilla extract
¼ teaspoon lemon extract
550 g strong plain flour

Preheat the oven to 180°C (350°F) Gas 4. Dissolve the yeast in 80 ml warm water in the bowl of a large mixer. Mix the potato flakes, 150 ml boiling water, sugar, butter and powdered milk in a separate bowl. Set aside to cool. When lukewarm, add this to the yeast mixture and stir to combine.

Add the eggs one at a time, then the salt, vanilla and lemon extract. Add the flour and mix well. Transfer to a large bowl and leave in a warm place until doubled in size, about 1 hour. When risen, form into your desired loaf shape and bake in the preheated oven for 45–55 minutes, until risen and golden brown.

Fresh Pineapple Flambé

SERVES 8–10

125 g butter
100 g soft brown sugar
½ pineapple, peeled, cored and cut into
    medium chunks
100–125 ml dark rum
8–10 Lace Cookie Cups (see right)
vanilla ice cream, to serve
edible flowers of your choice, to garnish (optional)

In a large frying pan, cook the butter and sugar over medium heat, stirring until the sugar is dissolved. Add the pineapple and

reduce the heat to low. Cook until the pineapple is browned on one side. Turn and cook until browned and soft. Carefully add the rum and set it alight.

Scoop vanilla ice cream into the lace cookie cups and spoon the cooked pineapple over the top. Drizzle with the rum liquid from the pan, garnish with a chunk of pineapple and a flower, if using, and serve immediately.

LACE COOKIE CUPS

1 quantity Lace Cookies (see page 41) with
    2 tablespoons sesame seeds
a 12-hole muffin tin or 10 individual moulds, lightly
    oiled or greased

Follow the method for making Lace Cookies on page 41 but sprinkle the cookies with sesame seeds before putting them in the oven. When the cookies are baked, but still warm, place each one into the prepared tin and use your fingers to press into the mould to form a cup shape. When cool, gently tip the cookie cups out. Use the cups as an edible serving dish for Fresh Pineapple Flambé (see left) or any flavour ice cream with the sauce of your choice. The cookies will keep for up to 1 week stored in an airtight container.

Passion Fruit Crème Brûlée

SERVES 8–10

12 large egg yolks
160 g granulated sugar
1 vanilla pod, halved lengthways
960 ml double cream, chilled
a pinch of salt
120 g ready-made passion fruit purée
8–12 teaspoons demerara sugar
slices of fresh fig and/or kiwi, to garnish (optional)
8–10 ramekins
a deep baking dish

Preheat the oven to 150°C (300°F) Gas 2. Mix the egg yolks and granulated sugar in a large bowl until combined. Slice the vanilla pod lengthways and scrape out the seeds with the back of a knife. Add the seeds and

pod to the double cream. Heat the cream and vanilla to scalding point, then gradually pour into the egg mixture while beating constantly. Add the salt and passion fruit purée. Pour the mixture through a sieve.

Divide the custard into ramekins and put them in a deep baking dish. Fill the baking dish with hot water three-quarters of the way up the sides of the ramekins. Bake in the preheated oven or 25–35 minutes.

Remove from the oven and leave to cool to room temperature, then refrigerate until well chilled. When ready to serve, spread an even layer of demerara sugar over the top of each custard. Caramelize with a blowtorch or place under a preheated grill for 3–4 minutes, until the sugar has caramelized and formed a topping.

Garnish with slices of fresh fig or kiwi, if using, and serve at room temperature.

Floral Tips

Flowers make people happy – plain and simple. If we surround ourselves with beautiful flowers we tend to feel better. It is a universal truth. Combining them well, however, is an art.

Floral Tips

USING COLOUR

Let's face it. Not everybody has good colour sense. For inexperienced floral designers one of the best rules is to design your arrangement with one colour even if you mix types of flowers. With all white flowers you can easily succeed in making a beautiful arrangement. If you really feel adventurous, add a dash of green. If you are newly venturing into colour, first try all pink or all red but feel free to vary the shades. If you want to use orange for instance, combine peach and apricot tones. Soon you will be expanding to mixing colours. When you do, it is best to stay with all pastels or all hot bright tones. Always think about your colour combinations. People respond to colour and it often has more impact than the type of flowers you use. With practice you will learn what combinations work. Floral designers are artists who 'paint' with colour.

TROPICAL FLOWERS

Tropical flowers stand alone beautifully. Ginger, heliconia, and bird of paradise are marvellously sculptural shapes that have strong impact on their own and don't need to be mixed with other flowers to be effective. They tend to be more expensive but you do not need as many stems to make a dramatic arrangement. A few tall or broad tropical leaves work well with these flowers and, in fact, their addition allows you to use even fewer blooms and reduce the cost. Many men who normally do not appreciate flowers that much still respond to the colours and drama offered by tropicals. It is best not to try to mix 'fluffy' or garden flowers with tropicals unless you are a more advanced designer. It is very tricky. The possible exception is orchids. Although orchids are 'tropical' flowers they work well with both tropical bouquets and traditional ones. Orchids combine quite nicely with roses. They also stand so beautifully on their own that a single stem in a vase is gorgeous.

ADD SOMETHING SURPRISING

Try to include something unusual and unexpected among your flowers or in the vase when you are designing an arrangement. An unusual bloom like a lotus blossom or some unnamed wild flower from

above Bright, hot colours mix
well and can generate strong,
happy feelings.

your garden can add a wonderful unexpected effect. Unusual elements in a floral arrangement invite closer attention. Exotic leaves, pods, berries, fruit or even vegetables are a nice touch. Filling your clear vase with shells, rocks or small fruit like kumquats is a nice but easy touch. A few asparagus or artichokes mixed with your flowers can be totally unexpected and delightful. Line or wrap your container with large leaves or tie your bouquet into a nosegay and drop it into your vase for an interesting change. You can even submerge certain blooms completely in water in a clear vase and amaze your friends with your ingenuity.

ONE FLOWER

There are certain flowers that are naturally so lovely or fascinating – or rare – that they do not need to be mixed with other blooms. Some of these are the ones that have the shortest seasons, like everybody's favourite peonies. Then there is lilac, lily of the valley, calla lilies or the multitudinous varieties of unusual garden roses. Some flowers like tulips and narcissus are at their most beautiful when gathered together in a mass with nothing added. A bouquet of white narcissus. An armful of sunflowers. A bundle of hydrangea. A fistful of violets. In each season nothing can surpass the beauty of these blooms. Of course that is not to say that you do not ever want to include these in a mixed bouquet. Peonies added to lilac or hydrangea added to a mixed bouquet of roses and tulips can be quite breathtaking.

GREEN

Green goes with just about anything although you do need to pay some attention to the shade of green you mix with other colours. Green is a trendy colour for flowers now, especially the hotter more acid shades, so growers are developing great tones of green flowers such as Jade and Green Tea roses, green cymbidium orchids, various shades of green hydrangea, and deep saturated green trachyllium. A little bit of acid green can spark many other colours. It makes pinks, browns and oranges really come alive. It adds wonderful depth and dimension to a mixed arrangement. If you don't have green flowers, drop a few limes into your vase and it can serve the same purpose.

above Pinks and pastels can project feminine and youthful qualities.

opposite page, top left

Tropical flowers are best mixed with other tropicals.

opposite page, top right

Unusual elements like poppy pods and lotus pods add a surprise touch.

opposite page, bottom left

There is nothing more beautiful than a vase of peonies on their own.

opposite page, bottom right

Green flowers and leaves combine naturally with any other colour.

SMALL THINGS TO CONSIDER

* If you are intimidated when you look at an empty vase, try gathering the flowers together in your hand and make a nosegay. Tie it together, cut the stems to one length and drop the entire bouquet into a vase.

*Use a vase with a small mouth that holds your flowers close together. It is easier to design than using a wide mouth vase that requires more flowers and allows excessive movement of the stems.

* For larger mouth vases, use florist tape to make a grid across the top of your vase to help hold the flowers upright. Otherwise, twist some curly willow or vines in the bottom of the vase to hold the stems in place.

* Sometimes it is easier and just as effective to make a variety of small vases to be placed around the house or gathered together in a grouping on your dining table. Use containers that are about 12–15 cm tall and not more than 15 cm wide. It is fun to mix different sizes and shapes. Look through your cupboards to find unusual containers like teapots, jugs or decorative drinking glasses.

* Think about adding some texture like berries, greenery or pods to your arrangement. Big flowers like hydrangea not only add texture but fill space and help to hold your other flowers in place.

* To help your flowers last longer, clean your vase with bleach to remove all bacteria and fill it with cold or room temperature water. Floral nutrients can help prolong their life. Cut stems at an angle. Woody stems like lilac are best if hammered and broken at the ends to facilitate absorbing water. Always keep flowers in a cool place, away from heat and out of direct sunshine. Change the water each day.

* When selecting flowers for entertaining buy them early enough to open fully the day of your party but do not buy them too early as they will be past their prime. Do the arrangements a day ahead so you do not need to worry about them on the day.

Business Credits

RENTALS

CHAMELEON CHAIR
4910 B West Rosecrans Ave.
Hawthorne, California 90250, USA
Tel: (+1) 310-973-8200
www.chameleonchair.com

CLASSIC PARTY RENTALS
2310 E Imperial Hwy.
El Segundo, California 90245, USA
Tel: (+1) 310-535-3660
www.classicpartyrentals.com

JACKSON SHRUB SUPPLY
11505 Vanowen St.
North Hollywood, California 91605, USA
Tel: (+1) 818-982-0100

TOWN & COUNTRY RENTALS
7700 Airport Business Park Way
Van Nuys, California 91406, USA
Tel: (+1) 818-908-4211
www.townandcountryrentals.com

LINENS

BBJ LINENS
Tel: (+1) 866-462-2552
www.bbjlinen.com

RESOURCE ONE
Los Angeles, USA
Tel: (+1) 818-343-3451
www.resourceone.info

RUTH FISCHL
New York City, USA
Tel: (+1) 212-273-9710
www.ruthfischl.com

CHINA & SILVER TABLEWARE

HERMÉS OF PARIS
434 No. Rodeo Drive, Beverly Hills,
California 90210, USA
Tel: (+1) 310-278-0890
www.hermes.com

TRACY PORTER Pottery
c/o Zrike Company Inc., USA
info@zrike.com

PLACE CARDS

LEHR & BLACK
8921 West Pico Blvd.
Los Angeles, California 90025, USA
Tel: (+1) 310-278-8182
www.lehrandblack.com

ANTIQUES & ACCESSORIES

LIEF
646 No. Almont, West Hollywood,
California 90069, USA
Tel: (+1) 310-492-0033

REVELRY EVENT DESIGN
Los Angeles, California, USA
Tel: (+1) 323-931-1880
www.revelryllc.com

SAN ANTONIO WINERY
737 Lamar St., Los Angeles,
California 90031, USA
www.sanantoniowinery.com

FOOD PRODUCTS

FISH KING
Jon Kagawa
722 No. Glendale Ave.
Glendale, California 91206, USA

PREMIER MEAT COMPANY
Andy Rocker
5030 Gifford Ave., Vernon,
California 90058, USA
Tel: (+1) 323-277-5888
www.premiermeats.com

Picture Credits

Page 2, 12 below both, 60–67, 124–131
The home of **Carol & Warner Henry**
designed by Barry Berkus, landscaped
design by Walt Young. Wines kindly
provided by the Henry Wine Group
www.henrywinegroup.com

Pages 42–49, 184, 185, 187, 192
Los Angeles residence designed by **David Vessey**
Vessey Design, INC.
Tel: (+1) 213 952 0103

Pages 68–75, 132–139
Joe Ruggiero, Furniture & Fabric designer
www.joeruggiero.com

Page 6, 14, 148–155
Mr. and Mrs. Robert J. Sutcliffe
Gardens of 'Little Court'
Pasadena, California

Pages 26–33, 164–171
The **Suz Rubel** family residence
designed by Karin Blake

Pages 12al 108–115
The home of **Taylor and Peggy Dark**

Pages 12ar, 84–91, 92–99, 116–123, 156–163
Tony Duquette's 'Dawnridge'
Tony Duquette Studios Ltd
P.O.Box 69858
West Hollywood, CA 90069

Pages 4–5, 11, 16–25
Estate of **Harry & Virginia Robinson**
and the L.A. County Park & Recreation
Virginia Robinson Gardens
1008 Elden Way
Beverley Hills, CA 90210
Tel: (+1) 310-276-5367
Fax: (+1) 310-276-5352
www.robinson-gardens.com

Index

In Appreciation

With special gratitude to Noelle Brown and Florence Brown for their constant encouragement and support and for opening the door to our first book and to Christina Held for keeping us organized and on track, as always. Thank you to Hans Boer for searching the world for our gorgeous flowers, Daniel Dreyer of Hermes and Danielle Waldman of Stephen Young Co. for helping us obtain many of our beautiful table settings and Loree Valle for loaning us her vintage California pottery. Thank you to our wonderful clients and especially those who generously offered their heartwarming comments for these pages and those who opened their homes to us for photography. And special gratitude to our incredible team of Mark's Garden floral designers who contributed to these parties: Luis 'Cesar' Martinez, Vinnie Bui, Marco Calderon, Anselmo 'Manny' Cosmes, Greg Delossantos, Jesus Felipe-Frausto, Owen Foster, Shahnaz Hanasab, Abraham Hernandez, Jose "Frankie" Hernandez, Lourdes Holguin, Anna Mayer, Leo Moreno, Christine Scheer and Cindy Smith

Mark Held and Richard David
of Mark's Garden

Many thanks to my co-authors, Mark Held and Richard David for inviting me to participate in this book. Their glorious flowers and décor are an inspiration for The Kitchen to provide the finest of food and drink. Brent Sherman and Megan Slaughter were of immense help in the shepherding and display of the food for the photo shoots. Brent's drinks taste as delicious as they look and Megan's help with revising our recipes was excellent. Thank you to: Classic Party Rentals and Ken Antonioli, who generously provided the rental equipment which so enhanced the party photos. Jerry Kohl kindly loaned us his handsome glasses from Brighton Inc., for the Moroccan Party. Fran Bigelow, owner of Fran's Chocolates Ltd. for her excellent chocolates and yummy idea for the Chocolate Covered Figs. Mr. Bob Sutcliffe who graciously helped us with many details regarding the book. Our great clients who kindly allowed us to invade their beautiful homes and never complained. The Kitchen staff who did their usual fine job in preparation of the food and to whom I am always indebted. My husband, Taylor Dark and our family for their patience and love over these many years.

Peggy Dark
of The Kitchen